Editor-in-Chief and Founder:
 Lyndon H. LaRouche, Jr.
Editorial Board: *Lyndon H. LaRouche, Jr. , Helga
 Zepp-LaRouche, Robert Ingraham, Tony
 Papert, Gerald Rose, Dennis Small, Jeffrey
 Steinberg, William Wertz*
Co-Editors: *Robert Ingraham, Tony Papert*
Managing Editor: *Nancy Spannaus*
Technology: *Marsha Freeman*
Books: *Katherine Notley*
Ebooks: *Richard Burden*
Graphics: *Alan Yue*
Photos: *Stuart Lewis*
Circulation Manager: *Stanley Ezrol*

INTELLIGENCE DIRECTORS
Counterintelligence: *Jeffrey Steinberg, Michele
 Steinberg*
Economics: *John Hoefle, Marcia Merry Baker,
 Paul Gallagher*
History: *Anton Chaitkin*
Ibero-America: *Dennis Small*
Russia and Eastern Europe: *Rachel Douglas*
United States: *Debra Freeman*

INTERNATIONAL BUREAUS
Bogotá: *Miriam Redondo*
Berlin: *Rainer Apel*
Copenhagen: *Tom Gillesberg*
Houston: *Harley Schlanger*
Lima: *Sara Madueño*
Melbourne: *Robert Barwick*
Mexico City: *Gerardo Castilleja Chávez*
New Delhi: *Ramtanu Maitra*
Paris: *Christine Bierre*
Stockholm: *Ulf Sandmark*
United Nations, N.Y.C.: *Leni Rubinstein*
Washington, D.C.: *William Jones*
Wiesbaden: *Göran Haglund*

ON THE WEB
e-mail: eirns@larouchepub.com
www.larouchepub.com
www.executiveintelligencereview.com
www.larouchepub.com/eiw
Webmaster: *John Sigerson*
Assistant Webmaster: *George Hollis*
Editor, Arabic-language edition: *Hussein Askary*

EIR (ISSN 0273-6314) *is published weekly
(50 issues), by EIR News Service, Inc.,
P.O. Box 17390, Washington, D.C. 20041-0390.
(703) 777-9451 ext. 415*

European Headquarters: E.I.R. GmbH, Postfach
Bahnstrasse 9a, D-65205, Wiesbaden, Germany
Tel: 49-611-73650
Homepage: http://www.eirna.com
e-mail: eirna@eirna.com
Director: Georg Neudecker

Montreal, Canada: 514-461-1557
eir@eircanada.ca

Denmark: EIR - Denmark, Sankt Knuds Vej 11,
basement left, DK-1903 Frederiksberg, Denmark.
Tel.: +45 35 43 60 40, Fax: +45 35 43 87 57. e-mail:
eirdk@hotmail.com.

Mexico City: EIR, Sor Juana Inés de la Cruz 242-2
Col. Agricultura C.P. 11360
Delegación M. Hidalgo, México D.F.
Tel. (5525) 5318-2301
eirmexico@gmail.com

Copyright: ©2016 EIR News Service. All rights
reserved. Reproduction in whole or in part without
permission strictly prohibited.

Canada Post Publication Sales Agreement
#40683579

Postmaster: Send all address changes to *EIR*, P.O.
Box 17390, Washington, D.C. 20041-0390.

Signed articles in *EIR* represent the views of the authors,
and not necessarily those of the Editorial Board.

The Ideas Which
Are Changing History

EDITORIAL

The Ideas which Can Now Change The History of Man and the Universe

by William F. Wertz, Jr.

William F. Wertz, Jr., spoke as follows, as he opened the discussion on LaRouche PAC's Thursday, March 23, "Fireside Chat" Activists' Conference Call.

Good evening everyone. What I just wanted to start out with is the fact that 34 years ago today, March 23, 1983, Ronald Reagan spoke before the nation and announced his Strategic Defense Initiative; the crucial words that he expressed were as follows:

I call upon the scientific community, who gave us nuclear weapons, to turn their great talents to the cause of mankind and world peace, to give us the means of rendering these weapons impotent and obsolete.

Now the reason I'm raising this is that Lyndon La-Rouche was the actual author of the Strategic Defense Initiative (SDI), and was involved in negotiations on behalf of the Reagan Administration with the then Soviet Union to get the Soviet agreement to jointly develop the Strategic Defense Initiative so that, in fact, the SDI was not only to benefit just one country—ourselves, the United States—to the detriment of the Soviet Union, which clearly would not eliminate the danger of thermonuclear war, but rather, it was to be a joint project involving advanced physical principles, at the frontiers of science, which would also have major ramifications for the development of the global economy.

The reason that's important is because we are now at a crucial moment in world history where similar ideas developed by Lyndon LaRouche have the potential to actually be consolidated on a global level as a result of the initiatives taken by the Russians, the Chinese, the Indians; and by the fact that we now have a President of the United States who is moving away from British imperial policy, which has led us to one war after another, and he is moving towards what he himself has called the "American System" of economics. That school of American System was initiated by Alexander Hamilton. And it's been brought back into the public domain by the efforts of Lyndon LaRouche and his associates starting really from at least the 1970s.

I just want to very briefly outline where we stand in the fight for the American System, and to also emphasize that what we're seeing is the power of reason, the power of strategic ideas which are consonant with the nature of man as a creative species—the only one that we know of—and the power of those ideas to change the direction of humanity, and to ultimately change the direction of the Universe.

One of the ideas that Lyndon LaRouche and Helga LaRouche have advocated is the Eurasian Land-bridge, which then became the World Land-bridge, and that has been adopted by the Chinese in the form of the "One Belt, One Road" policy or the New Silk Road Initiative, and this concept is a concept which you can also trace back to the policy of Pope Paul VI, at the time he put forward an encyclical called, *Populorum Progressio*, where he said that "the new name of peace is development." This is the concept which Prime Minister Modi of India also recently put forward when he visited the United States and said we have to develop a "mass movement for development."

Development is the basis for world peace, and this is a concept which Lyndon LaRouche has put forward with scientific rigor, for decades. And that policy not only has become increasingly hegemonic as the trans-Atlantic region has become increasingly bankrupt, but I would say that we're on the verge of that policy not only becoming hegemonic, but actually consolidating itself on a global level, to the extent to which the United States is brought into that dynamic.

We have circulated a petition for some time, calling for the United States to join the BRICS. The BRICS nations are Brazil, Russia, India, China, and South Africa, which have been actually pushing this kind of policy. And under Obama, or had Hillary Clinton won the election, the United States joining that process would have been the furthest thing from reality, because their policy was the British policy of geopolitics, of war. I would say that we're on the verge of this policy of economic development, of the "One Belt, One Road" policy, coming into a position of consolidation.

As you may have heard, Secretary of State Rex Tillerson was recently in China. When he was there, he actually endorsed the policy formulation of President Xi of China. He said that "we agree with the policy of nonconfrontation, mutual respect, and win-win" as opposed to a zero-sum game, which is what geopolitics is. In other words, somebody wins, somebody loses—or everybody loses, in fact. But in fact, the Chinese are putting forward this perspective, and Tillerson endorsed that perspective.

There is a conference that will take place in Beijing on May 14 and 15, on the "One Belt, One Road." As many as 60 or more nations are expected to be there. President Trump has been invited to go there. That's a definite possibility, although there is no confirmation of that at this point. It is possible that there will be a summit between President Trump and President Xi in early April in the United States, and if that were to occur, that would probably mean that Trump would move in the direction of endorsing the One Belt, One Road policy.

As you may know, another Asian leader, Shinzo Abe from Japan, also recently came to the United States. He is working very closely with the Russians on economic development, and he made offers of invest-ment in the United States to help redevelop U.S. infrastructure, and there is potential that the Chinese would do the same as a result of the One Belt, One Road policy.

Bring Back Hamilton's System

Since March 15, President Trump has given three extraordinary speeches. One was in Michigan, where he talked about rebuilding the U.S. manufacturing base, building cities. He welcomed foreign investment in the United States. Then he went down to Louisville, Kentucky and gave another speech there, and I think the next day, he gave a speech in Washington, D.C. at the Republican Congressional Campaign Committee event. These speeches are not getting wide publicity in the mainstream media, but what he has called for is the American System of political economy. He has explicitly called for that. When he was in Kentucky, he referred to Abraham Lincoln, who was an advocate of the American System of economy. He referred to Henry Clay—he was basically going through a list of people who were born in Kentucky, including Lincoln who was born there, Henry Clay who was born there, among others. And the basic thing that he was saying was that we're going to develop the U.S. economy. We're going to develop manufacturing. We're going to put coal workers back to work. We're going to have auto plants back in Michigan and Kentucky. He rejected the idea of free trade, which is actually the British system policy of Adam Smith, as opposed to the American System of protectionism and what he called "fair trade" or "reciprocity."

Then in the speech in Washington, D.C., he went even further. He said that he advocated the "American model" of economy, the American System, which he said was what our Founders wanted, and he referred explicitly to Washington, to Alexander Hamilton, and also to Lincoln, again. He really emphasized the role of Lincoln and Eisenhower in developing the infrastructure of this country, and said that Republicans should be builders in that tradition. One of the things he referred to was the fact that Lincoln in 1832, in his first run for Congress, when he was merely 23 years old, had advocated bringing railroads to Illinois even though he had never seen a steam-powered engine. It was that campaign in 1823 which foreshadowed his later promotion of the Transcontinental Railroad in the 1860s. Similarly, he pointed out that after World War I, Eisenhower had participated in the first military convoy that traveled from Washington, D.C. to the Pacific on the Lincoln Highway, and that this experience on the part of Eisenhower led him to fight for and introduce the Interstate Highway system.

So, what you've got here is a President who does not have a fully rigorous, scientific understanding of the American System but who, as Lyndon LaRouche said, after having watched the Kentucky speech and the Washington, DC speech, is seriously committed to this perspective.

So what you have is a situation where the British system is collapsing. The hegemonic conception in the world right now is one of economic development, as expressed in the One Belt, One Road policy of the Chinese, which we, the LaRouche movement, have advocated for decades. And at the same time, you now have a President who is breaking from extreme environmentalism, who is breaking from British free-trade policies, who is breaking from a policy of regime change and geopolitics, and is willing to embrace the conception of "win-win" partnership, which also has a certain history in the United States and in Europe. This is the principle of the Treaty of Westphalia, which ended the 30 years of religious warfare in continental Europe back in the 1600s. The conception of that treaty was that you should have a foreign policy based on the advantage of the other—the concept of what in Greek, the Greek conception of love *agapē*. Of course, in the United States, John Quincy Adams put forward a conception of "community of principle among sovereign nations" as what our foreign policy should be, as opposed to the geopolitics of the British.

So we're in the situation where we have it within our hands to bring about a fundamental change in the nature of human society, and we really have a capability at this point of going beyond merely making proposals or complaining about the *status quo*—and actually winning. We're on the actual verge of winning to the extent to which we realize it and take that perspective.

We, in the LaRouche movement, particularly the Schiller Institute, are planning a major conference in New York City, April 14-15, on the Silk Road, and also on a dialogue of philosophies or cultures. This conference is a very important element in this dynamic in assuring it succeeds on the deepest level of understanding of the mission of humanity.

I would also point out that tomorrow, March 24, is the hundredth anniversary of one of the greatest pioneers of space science, Krafft Ehricke, a German scientist who came to the United States and was instrumental in the U.S. space program. He passed away early, in 1984, at the age of 67. His ideas about an "extraterrestrial imperative" have a certain consonance with the actual nature of man, which is now again on the verge of fruition, as more and more countries are committing themselves to space exploration. The Chinese are committed to a lunar program, including mining helium-3 on the Moon, which is a crucial element in terms of fusion energy. President Trump himself just signed a space bill, the first one we've had in a number of years, after Obama successfully took down much of our space program during the last eight years.

So, as you can imagine, the British are very freaked out about this. They have gone berserk prior to Trump's election and increasingly since his election, and I think we can discuss that further if people want to, but what Lyndon LaRouche said just the other day is "you have to understand—this is the British. The entire attack on Trump is the British." And, as he said, "it will not work."

EIR Contents

www.larouchepub.com Volume 44, Number 13, March 31, 2017

Cover This Week

Lyndon H. LaRouche, Jr.; Alexander Hamilton

I. The American System of Lyndon LaRouche

The Issue Today Is Lyndon LaRouche

by Michael G. Steger

March 28—In the aftermath of the Second World War, Western Civilization encountered a crossroads. The scientific, technological, and industrial levels attained by Franklin Roosevelt's application of the storied American System of Political Economy—a system established by first Treasury Secretary Alexander Hamilton, and under that name, last applied by William McKinley as part of Lincoln's Republican Party tradition—had taken mankind far, far beyond the industrial might of the first industrial revolution launched by Lincoln and his followers.

The power of the nucleus, the vast expanse of the the trillions of galaxies—all of which were awakened by Einstein's discoveries—when once integrated into the powers of the human economy, had launched mankind far beyond the confines of our planet. Visionary scientists such as Krafft Ehricke, who by the early 1930s were participating in advanced rocketry programs, were all governed by a mission to put man on the moon and beyond, and still their voices beckon us outward.

Franklin Roosevelt's Presidency took the most advanced sciences and technology—such as the electromagnetic principles developed by Einstein's German predecessors, e.g. Karl Gauss, Wilhelm Weber, and Bernhard Riemann, along with Einstein's own deeper insights into the micro-domain of the nucleus, and launched an entirely new domain of human evolutionary development. The broadscale application of this most advanced technology to every area of the nation, through projects such as the REA, TVA, and the Four

LPAC

Lyndon H. LaRouche, Jr.

Corners more generally, combined with machine-tool and manufacturing development, and in conjunction with the wartime Manhattan Project—a precursor to the peacetime Apollo Project, both of which served as a science driver project to master the most advanced scientific and technological frontiers—created the most irrefutable demonstration of the renowned American System of Political Economy ever seen.

It is for this very reason that FDR remains the scourge of Wall St. establishment political factions today.

More important, however, was the scientific advancement which stemmed from this evolutionary leap.

Lyndon LaRouche was raised within the era of Franklin Roosevelt's Presidency. By his early adolescence he had become a devoted adherent to the work of Gottfried Leibniz, the same Leibniz who was the inspiration for Gauss, Riemann, and Einstein, and was also the founder of the science of physical economy (as contrasted with the paltry accounting field of monetary economics so vaunted today).

During the early years immediately following the interruption of a long series of international wars in 1945, and while some brave souls within the United States chose to fight to keep FDR's American System alive—although they failed at that time under the onslaught of Truman's British schemes of Cold War and Red-scare hysteria—Mr. LaRouche, who was part of this fight, accomplished the most beautiful discovery of human society thus far known.

Real Presidential leadership: FDR at the dedication of the Boulder Dam on Sept. 30,1935.

(The reader should look to Mr. LaRouche's own writings to document the nature of his discovery, but nothing more beautiful has ever been discovered.)

This discovery eventually led Mr. LaRouche to establish the most successful political insurgency into international politics that modern history has ever seen. By 1983, Lyndon LaRouche and his associates, after starting on the streets of New York City in the 1960's, had emerged as a national, and international political and scientific force, shaping and inspiring Ronald Reagan's commitment to end the threat of nuclear war and launch a new era of Renaissance, beginning with the beam weapons defense program called the Strategic Defense Initiative (SDI).

Since the launch of the SDI the world has never been the same. The Cold War was ended, even if not in the delusions of the unfortunate species of British Agents such as Obama, Cheney, et al.

Today, China has emerged as the leading patron of this storied American System of Economy, largely through the efforts of Lyndon LaRouche, and his wife Helga, who, after the fall of Berlin Wall, brought this legacy of the Renaissance into the discussion of the leading Confucian political leaders of China, as China emerged as a modern nation.

Today, again, we find ourselves at that same crossroads, but with a different point of vantage—the vantage of having watched our own nation suffer the destruction, misery, drug addiction, despair, and confusion that all nations have faced under the boot of British imperialism/fascism, although for us, the face of imperial destruction wore the British Tavistock Institution's liberal smile, such as with Obama, to an extent that was perhaps never seen before.

The relations of the United States and China present a great opportunity. The relations between the United States, Russia, and China, in friendship, represent the cornerstone of a world system without empire, one based potentially, and necessarily, on that most beautiful discovery of Lyndon LaRouche.

There is now a great moment before us, as President Trump revives the American System, as no other President has done, under that name, since William McKinley did so. And with the discovery by Mr. LaRouche, who along with his associates revived the American System out of the history books and into the fight for control of the Presidency since 1976, the American System can be revived with even greater scientific efficacy than it was under Franklin Roosevelt.

We find ourselves at a great crossroads. The issue at hand, is the issue of the truth—the truth of mankind's future. That truth is expressed no more distinctly than in the life of Lyndon LaRouche.

For there is a no more critical factor to unleash the greatest Renaissance mankind has ever seen, than to acknowledge the true source of discovery by which that Renaissance was made possible. As with Brunelleschi and Cusa, who inspired the Florentine Renaissance, or with Kepler, who built his dome from the starry heavens—a discovery which Isaac Newton could never understand.

Today, Lyndon LaRouche is not only the architect of a new dome built from the fabric of the entirety of human culture, and one built for all mankind to grasp and build upon—he is also the leading figure in the American System of Political Economy.

The necessary immediate steps must now be taken to ensure the most advanced development of the American System.

An elimination of the British System, the end of the Wall St. failed banks, and a special elimination of the fascist wing of the F.B.I,, as we see operating against the Trump Administration today—the same F.B.I. which targeted Lyndon LaRouche for personal destruction because of the implications and power of his discovery—is the immediate place to start.

On the Cusp of a New World: The Import of President Trump's Four Recent Interventions

by Robert Ingraham

March 26—The Anglo-American elites are now leading "get-Trump" operations intended to destroy the Trump Administration and to drive Donald Trump—by whatever means required—from office. A comprehensive, devastating exposé by Barbara Boyd is featured in this issue of *EIR*.

Printed below are extended excerpts from three recent speeches by President Trump. One need not look any further to understand the murderous hatred of the President by the Anglo-American establishment, than just what is expressed in those speeches. The President, from the standpoint of London and Wall Street, is committing an unpardonable sin—a "sin unto death." He is explicitly referencing and reviving those principles and policies which have historically separated and distinguished the United States of America from the murderous legacy of the British Empire. He is threatening the very existence of the policies and philosophies which have controlled the nation since the murder of John F. Kennedy. He is speaking truths which have not been publicly uttered in decades by any leading elected official. And he is educating and rallying the American people for the fight ahead.

Make no mistake. We are

NASA

Astronaut Ed White became the first first American to walk in Space on June 3, 1965, during NASA's Gemini 4 mission.

at a great historical inflection point. In addition to the three speeches delivered by President Trump between March 15 and March 21, on March 25 he made a fourth intervention. In his regular Weekly Address, the President devoted the entire, extraordinary broadcast to his intention to revive America's space program. He stated:

> My fellow Americans—this week, in the company of astronauts, I was honored to sign the NASA Transition Authorization Act right into law. With this legislation, we renew our national commitment to NASA's mission of exploration and discovery. And we continue a tradition that is as old as mankind. We look to the heavens with wonder and curiosity. ... NASA's greatest discoveries teach us many, many things. One lesson is the need to view old questions with fresh eyes, to have the courage to look for answers in places we have never looked before. To think in new ways because we have new information. Most of all, new discoveries remind us that, in America, anything is possible if we have the courage and wisdom to learn.

As you will see in the three speeches—all of which address the central issue of rebuilding American manufacturing, infrastructure, and science policy—the President explicitly names Alexander Hamilton and Abraham Lincoln as the model for his approach, and he additionally references Dwight Eisenhower, Henry Clay, and implicitly, William McKinley.

At the speeches in Washington and Michigan, the President names his economic approach the "American Model," a term which echos the Nineteenth Century "American System" of economics. And if one examines the clear message contained within those speeches, as well as in the Weekly Address of March 25, a Hamiltonian intention is explicit.

In the estimation of Lyndon LaRouche, President Trump "meant it." He truly wants to return to the actual economic policies of Alexander Hamilton, George Washington, and Abraham Lincoln.

This is now our fight—to win or lose. The surest pathway to success—for President Trump and the nation—were for the President to "heed the wise words of Lyndon LaRouche," the premier Hamiltonian economist of the last one hundred years. In his "Four New Laws to Save the U.S.A.," LaRouche has defined the precise Hamiltonian principles and policies which will ensure that the intention enunciated by President Trump succeeds—and that a new productive future for all of humanity is realized.

Library of Congress

Ford's Willow Run bomber plant turned out one B-24 heavy bomber per hour (up to 25 per day) during World War II.

March 15

President Trump Speech at
The American Center for Mobility, Willow Run, Mich.

The President: Our great Presidents, from Washington to Jefferson to Jackson to Lincoln, all understood that a great nation must protect its manufacturing, must protect itself from the outside. Today, I will be visiting the home of Andrew Jackson on the 250th anniversary of his birth. And they say my election was most similar to his—1828. That's a long time ago. Usually they go back like to this one, or that one, 12 years ago, 16. I mean, 1828, that's a long way. That's a long time ago...

We must embrace a new economic model. Let's call it "The American Model."

Under this system, we will reduce burdens on our companies and on our businesses. But, in exchange, companies must hire and grow in America. They have to hire and grow in our country. That is how we will succeed and grow together—American workers and American industry side-by-side. Nobody can beat us, folks. Nobody can beat us. Because whether we are rich or poor, young or old, black or brown or white, we all bleed the same red blood of patriots...

Great Americans of all backgrounds built the Arsenal of Democracy—including the legendary Rosie the Riveter, who worked here at Willow Run. You know that. Seventy-five years ago, during the Second World War, thousands of American workers filled this very building to build the great new airplanes—the B-24 Liberator. At peak production—listen to this—it's not the country that we've been watching over the last 20 years—they were building one B-24 every single hour. We don't hear that. We don't hear that any more, do we? We'll be back. We'll be back soon. Most amazing people. ...

Now, these hundreds of acres that defended our democracy are going to help build the cars and cities of the future... so I ask you today to join me in daring to believe that this facility, this city, and this nation will once again shine with industrial might.

I am asking you to place your faith in the American worker and these great American companies. I'm also asking you to respect and place your faith in companies from foreign lands that come here to build their product. We love them too, right? We love them too.

I'm asking all of the companies here today to

join us in this new Industrial Revolution. Let us put American workers, American families, and American dreams first once again.

May God bless the American worker. May God bless the Motor City. And may God bless the United States of America. Thank you.

March 20

President Trump Speech
**at
Make America Great
Again Rally, Freedom
Hall, Louisville, Ky.**

California Governor Leland Stanford pounds in the ceremonial golden spike in Promontory, Utah, on May 10, 1869, that completes the nation's first transcontinental railway.

The President: I am thrilled to be here in the great state of Kentucky and the beautiful city of Louisville! And this place is packed. There are a lot of people outside that aren't getting in, but that's all right. We love them, too, right? We love them, too.

We're in the heartland of America, and there is no place I would rather be than here with you, tonight. Our first Republican President, Abraham Lincoln, was born right here in Kentucky. That's not bad. The legendary pioneer, Daniel Boone, helped settle the Kentucky frontier. And the great Nineteenth Century American statesman, Henry Clay, represented Kentucky in the United States Congress. Henry Clay believed in what he called the *American System,* and proposed tariffs to protect American industry, and finance American infrastructure...

Clay was a fierce advocate for American manufacturing. He wanted it badly. He said, very strongly: Free trade, which would throw wide open our ports to foreign production without duties, while theirs remains closed to us. That was his quote. He knew, all the way back, early 1800s. Clay said that trade must be fair, equal, and reciprocal. Boom. He said, fair, equal, and reciprocal. I'm talking about reciprocal trade. Reciprocal. ...

In explaining his American System, Clay argued that the sole object of the tariff is to tax the produce and—remember, to tax the produce of foreign industry with the view of promoting American industry. For too long, our government has abandoned the American system. Since NAFTA was approved in 1994—the worst trade deal ever made by any country I think in the world—America has lost nearly one-third of its manufacturing jobs. Do not worry, we are starting on NAFTA very soon.
...

So with hope in our souls, and patriotism in our hearts, let us now recite these words. Are you ready? Together, we will make America strong again. We will make America wealthy again. We will make America proud again. We will make safe again. And we will make America great again. Thank you. Thank you, Kentucky. God bless you.

March 21

President Trump Speech **to the National Republican Congressional Committee Dinner, National Building Museum, Washington, D.C.**

The President: I have called this model, the model that you've been watching, the model that's created so much value, the model of bringing back jobs and bringing back industry—I called it the *American Model.* And this is the system that our Founders wanted. Our greatest American leaders—including George Washington, Hamilton, Jackson, Lincoln—they all agreed that for America to be a strong nation it must also be a great manufacturing nation...

The Republican platform of 1896—more than a century ago—stated that: "Protection and reciprocity are twin measures of American policy and go hand in hand." I mean, we have situations where other countries who have zero respect for our country ... will tax us 100 percent tax on some—100 percent! And we charge them nothing. They'll make it impossible through regulations for our product to be sold in their country, and yet they'll sell their product routinely in our country. Not going to happen any more. . . .

The word, "reciprocity"—they do it, we do it. Who can complain about that?

. . . The platform went on to say: "We renew and emphasize our allegiance to the policy of protection, as the bulwark of American industrial independence and the foundation of American development and prosperity. . . ."

Our first Republican President, Abraham Lincoln, ran his first campaign for public office in 1832—when he was only 23 years old. He began by imagining the benefits a railroad could bring to his part of Illinois—without ever having seen a steam-powered train. He had no idea, and yet he knew what it could be. Thirty years later, as President, Lincoln signed the law that built the first Transcontinental Railroad, uniting our country from ocean to ocean. Great President. Most people don't even know he was a Republican, right? Does anyone know?

. . . Another great Republican President, Dwight Eisenhower, had a vision of a national infrastructure plan. As an officer in the Army after World War I, he joined a military convoy that trekked across the nation to the Pacific Coast. It traveled along the Lincoln Highway—called then the Lincoln Highway. Its journey began by the South Lawn of the White House, at a monument known today as Zero Milestone. Anybody know where that is? The journey made a great impression on the then young Eisenhower. More than three decades later, as President, he signed the bill that created our great Interstate Highway System—once again uniting us as a nation.

Now is time for a new Republican administration, working with our Republican Congress, to pass the next great infrastructure bill. Our party must dream as big and as bold as Lincoln and Eisenhower. Together, Republicans will lead America into our unbelievable future. We have so much potential. We have so much potential. I see it now even more than I saw it in this great campaign—which turned out to be a movement, a movement like the world has never seen before, actually.

Imagine the breakthroughs that will breathe fresh life into forgotten places. Picture the new roads that will carve pathways all across our land— and we need them. And think of the new inventions that will lift up the sights of our nation. . .

The best Republican Presidents have not only been war-fighters, but also peacemakers. We will never hesitate to do what we must to keep us safe today, but we will always seek a more peaceful tomorrow. We will, and we will succeed.

If we stand for these things—safety, prosperity and peace—then there is no limit to what we can achieve: A future where millions are lifted from welfare to work. And they're going to love it. They're going to love it. They're going to love waking up in the morning, going to work. Communities thriving with jobs and surging with commerce. Inner cities filled with new hope and new opportunity. Schools where our children can learn free from violence and free from fear. And new frontiers in science, technology, and space that inspire the next generation of American youth.

All of this, and so much more, is possible. Our country is great. A new national pride is stirring our souls. A new optimism is sweeping our land. A new era of American greatness is just beginning.

Somewhere in America tonight, a child is born in poverty, looking up into the sky, and filling their heart with dreams—big, beautiful, bold dreams. And if we make the right choices together, then no one will ever have to tell that child that their dreams will have to wait for another day, another year, or another decade. Because the waiting now is over. The time for action is now. This is the moment when great deeds are done—and we will do those great deeds. By putting our faith in the people, and by putting our trust in God, we will rise to this occasion like no one has ever risen before.

We will prove worthy of this moment. Anything is possible if we stand together, united and strong. Not just as Republicans—but as great and unified Americans. Join me in believing in this better and brighter future. Join me in building this reality. And join me in rededicating ourselves to the common good of this nation that we all love so much. Together, we will defend our freedoms. We will defend our people. . . .

Thank you. God bless you, and God bless the United States of America. Thank you very much.

Every Day Counts In Today's Showdown To Save Civilization

That's why you need EIR's **Daily Alert Service**, a strategic overview compiled with the input of Lyndon LaRouche, and delivered to your email 5 days a week.

The election of Donald Trump to the Presidency of the Untied States has launched a new global era whose character has yet to be determined. The Obama-Clinton drive toward confrontation with Russia has been disrupted--but what will come next?

Over the next weeks and months there will be a pitched battle to determine the course of the Trump Administration. Will it pursue policies of cooperation with Russia and China in the New Silk Road, as the President-Elect has given some signs of? Will it follow through against Wall Street with Glass-Steagall?

The opposition to these policies will be fierce. If there is to be a positive outcome to this battle, an informed citizenry must do its part--intervening, educating, inspiring. That's why you need the EIR Daily Alert more than ever.

TUESDAY, NOVEMBER 22, 2016

Volume 3, Number 65

EIR Daily Alert Service

P.O. Box 17390, Washington, DC 20041-0390

- Only Global Solutions, Based on New Principles, Can Work
- Tulsi Gabbard Meets with Donald Trump Regarding Syria
- Robert Kagan Throws in the Towel, Complains U.S. Is Becoming 'Solipsistic'
- War Party Moving To Preempt Trump-Putin Reset
- Syrian Army Makes More Progress in Aleppo
- Duterte Gives OK to Nuclear Power for Philippines
- Europe Will Suffer from Maintaining Russia Sanctions
- Former Chilean Diplomat Confirmed, 'We Will Joyfully Welcome Xi Jinping'
- Duterte and Putin Establish Philippines-Russia Cooperation
- François Fillon, Pro-Russian Thatcherite, Wins First Round of French Right-Wing Presidential Primary

EDITORIAL

Only Global Solutions, Based on New Principles, Can Work

The Insurrection Against the President, And Its British Controllers—Or, Who Really Is George Soros, Anyway?

by Barbara Boyd

March 21—A frantic effort by British Empire imperialists is now fully underway in the United States and internationally. It aims to crush the *potential*, represented by the Trump Presidency, a potential which could consign these elites and their murderous post-World War II "New World Order" to the dustbin of history. This is the strategic analysis of Lyndon LaRouche, who has studied and analyzed the machinations of this grouping for decades.

Against the screams daily emanating from their controlled media and the men and women of Davos, an actual engine for economic growth has been unleashed on the world by China, in an alliance with Russia and India, joined most recently by Japan. Unleashing a wave of hope throughout the developing world, this alliance could, if joined by the United States, usher in a new boundless human renaissance.

Since September 2013, China has undertaken a huge infrastructure-building project, ripe with the potential to transform entire underdeveloped, forsaken, or war ravaged areas of the Earth into modern, beautiful cities and productive economies. This grand design of great projects, for which Lyndon LaRouche has campaigned internationally for more than forty years, is now being built. It is the largest worldwide infrastructure project ever undertaken by human beings. Russia, China, and India are also turning their imaginations to near space exploration, intent on exploring and developing the moon where, among other wonders, the possibility for rapid development of fusion energy to power the Earth and future space travel beckons.

China's President Xi Jinping asked the United States to join this effort; Barack Obama adamantly refused, opting instead for a series of hostile actions which can only be described as a New Cold War.

The enemies of global development—and now the enemies of President Donald Trump—have been called the "Deep State" by Trump's allies. We prefer not to elevate their incompetence, corruption, and failed policies in this report. We refer to them, instead, as the **"Blimps"**—short for British Liberal Imperialists.

These are the bankers of Wall Street and the City of London, allied with old European dynasties, particularly Queen Elizabeth's House of Windsor, who brought Hitler and Mussolini to power on behalf of the British geopolitical goal of conquering Eurasia, starting with Russia. When that failed, they first played with the idea of dropping a nuclear bomb on the Soviet Union and then

White House Photo

President Trump delivering his first message to a Joint Session of Congress, Feb. 28, 2017.

launched the Cold War "containment" policy announced by Winston Churchill at Fulton, Missouri on March 5, 1946.[1] After the fall of the Soviet Union, they looted Russia and all the other former Soviet states. Now that a true Russian leader has emerged again, they are ringing Russia with hostile states, many of them created by "color revolutions," and new-generation nuclear weapons, which the Russians and many informed scientists in the United States rightly believe, could represent a "First Strike" capability.[2] Thus, the world sits on the hair-trigger for thermonuclear war.

After Franklin Roosevelt's death, the Blimps destroyed classical culture, the spark for the development of human creative genius, in the name of the Cold War. They dismantled the economy which Roosevelt had built, touting the exercise as "controlled disintegration," and left in its wake the post-industrial rubble of the so-called gig and information economy, dominated by drugs, reality television, violent video games, gangsta rap, and magical thinking.

As of this writing, voters in the United States, in Britain, and in Italy, have decisively rejected the Blimps' twin nostrums of free trade and globalism, alleged to be the civil-society foundations of all modern "democratic" states. Since the financial crisis of 2008, the Blimps have simply continued and expanded their savage assault against the living standards of their populations and the laws of physical economic progress, while enriching themselves. Their doomed financial system could blow up at any moment, unleashing unimaginable and worldwide social chaos. The idea that Donald Trump would join the United States with Russia, China, and India in a new paradigm for economic development, is seen, correctly, by them, as a deadly threat to their existence.

That said, the worldwide freak-out of the elites over Trump is fairly unprecedented for living generations. Put simply, the Blimps have openly threatened to kill Trump and go to war against what they see as the emergent threat against them from what China, Russia, India, and Japan are accomplishing in Eurasia. Newspapers in both Germany and Britain—*Die Zeit* and the *Spectator*—have openly opined that Trump will (and must) be removed by any means necessary, even if it

The lead feature article in the London Spectator *on Jan. 21, 2017, the day after President Trump's inauguration.*

means assassination. Such talk is said to now be routine on the Washington, D.C. cocktail party circuit. Various Hollywood figures, including the appropriately named Snoop Dogg, have pantomimed the President's assassination in widely circulated snuff videos.

And, as Trump said in a television interview recently (sending the Blimps into a rage fit), they have killed, repeatedly, since Franklin Roosevelt's death.

The most recent and coldly "professional" illustration of this practice is Barack Obama. Armed with "baseball card profiles" of alleged terrorists, provided by his would-be grand inquisitor, the ghoulish[3] John Brennan, Obama engaged in ritual killings by drone every Tuesday afternoon, bragging that he was "good at it." Brennan's competence, in providing profiles for America's first President to routinely act as summary executioner, can be gauged by the fact that he spent much of his career in the CIA as the gopher for George Tenet. Tenet is the guy who claimed that Saddam Hussein had weapons of mass destruction, calling that conclusion a "slam dunk." Such is the criminal mind of the Blimps.

---

1. Churchill borrowed the phrase, "Iron Curtain," not so accidentally, from Nazi propagandist Joseph Goebbels who also used it to refer to the Soviet Union.

2. See, e.g., Jonathan Marshall, "Dreams of Winning a Nuclear War with Russia," *Consortium News*, March 10, 2017.

---

3. The term "ghoul" was defined by the great American poet, Edgar Allen Poe, as a "pestilential carcass departed from a soul." Were he alive today, Poe would certainly use the term to describe both Brennan and Obama.

The Blimps have also unleashed their entire modern black-propaganda apparatus, dating from the post-World War I interval, in the hopes of suckering the masses into an enraged "color revolution" against the President, all under the tutelage of the color revolution-trained activists and Democratic Leadership Council-spawned "thought" leaders, who took over the Democratic Party fully after Barack Obama's 2008 campaign.

To defeat them, we Americans need to learn our own suppressed revolutionary history, particularly the principles contained within the Public Credit System enunciated by Alexander Hamilton, and the modern scientific enrichment of those principles as developed by Lyndon LaRouche over the last forty-five years. These are the proven principles which have served America for more than two centuries. These ideas drove the sustained economic and scientific progress found in Hamilton's early United States, during the Lincoln Administration, and during the recovery and war mobilization led by Roosevelt. They were fundamentally advanced by LaRouche's breakthrough discoveries providing the scientific metrics for sustained economic and social progress. They are encapsulated in LaRouche's *Four Laws for Economic Recovery*.

We also must exploit the two glaring vulnerabilities of the decadent, post-World War II "New World Order," created by the Blimps.

John McCain cites Trump's violations of that "Order" as the *casus belli* for the insurrection now underway against the President.[4] The chief vulnerability of that Order is its complete disregard for the fundamental laws of physical economic science. Addicted to monetary gambling, it simply does not know how to build an economy capable of sustained social and economic progress. It banks its survival on continued enslavement of subject populations through propaganda, dumbed-down education, entertainment, drugs, and perpetual wars. Like Rome—the imperial model for this modern-day British Empire—it is doomed to fail. The issue is whether the entire human race vanishes with it in a nuclear catastrophe.

---

4. Mad Senator John McCain recently rambled that in his loutish actions against Donald Trump, he was leading a defense of nothing less than the post-World War II "New World Order." In the same set of interviews, at Davos, the yearly gabfest of the elites, his delusional buddy, Senator Lindsey Graham, like the Queen of Hearts in Alice in Wonderland, snarled about kicking "Russian ass." Appropriately, the President has implored the Bobbsey Twins of thermonuclear destruction to shut up, tweeting: "Stop trying to start World War III."

The second vulnerability is found in the criminal anti-human history of the New World Order itself. If understood fully by the population—if the smoke and mirrors magic show stops—the Blimps are doomed. This short primer aims to be the first step in an urgent educational process.

I. President Trump and the Deep State, a.k.a. the Modern British Empire

Breitbart has been running a tongue-in-cheek series under the byline "Virgil" featuring minutes of the "Deep State's" permanent campaign against Donald Trump. It envisions a Deep State Central Committee, a guerilla division of protesters, a media division, a culture division, and so on. While simplistic and satirical, it is not wrong.

The Deep State, as defined by the writers who actually created the term, is the post-World War II entity consisting of Wall Street and London's banks and law firms, the state intelligence agencies they created and staffed, controlled corporate media, foundations, and think-tanks—a structure which intersects organized crime and certain sponsored politicians. It produces "deep" and universally destabilizing events in society, such as the assassination of John F. Kennedy, from which it apparently emerges unscathed.

Since Franklin Roosevelt's death, this entity's credo has been neoliberalism, a nihilistic, godless "philosophy" which promotes existentialism, pessimism, and a form of "freedom" which amounts to nothing more than personal narcissism, whether it be in the form of Ayn Rand's "egotism" or the self-realization mantras of the professional class. Having killed God, the random "free market" is alleged to reign over and determine the affairs of human beings. It seeks open borders (so that human labor can be had at the lowest possible wage) and free trade (so that goods might be produced at the cheapest price without regard to developing the economy or labor). That philosophy is otherwise embodied in Barack Obama's imperial dictum: "We set the rules," and in the failed economic nostrums of Friedrich von Hayek, Ludwig von Mises, and Milton Friedman.

Shortly after World War I, the Anglo-American elite set out to control the world *through the manipulation of public opinion and associated models of fake democracy*. The American Century Project envisioned by

Henry Luce set out various models of socially engineered control of the population, all of them conducted under the claim that the population was democratically "choosing" its fate.[5] This is a modern update of the ancient oligarchic model of society in which an elite continually plunders a backward population. Imagine, if you will, a lizard, a venomous Gila Monster which is able to change its colors, like a chameleon. Hitler, for example, conducted popular referenda to support his earliest controversial proposals. Today, George Soros' "Open Society," by reducing the world to small "communitarian" enclaves which replicate a feudal system, is but the latest version of the monster.

CNN screen capture

CNN played a leading role in spreading the view that it is a cardinal sin to negotiate with Russia.

The United States, despite what you learned in school, was never intended to be a pure democracy. Our forefathers attacked that idea as nothing better than dictatorship by mob, the types of mobs which they had seen repeatedly manipulated by the British Empire. Our Constitution stipulates that we are a Republic, in which an educated and engaged citizenry is supposed to deliberate on the policies of government through elected representatives, in a dialogue led by the President and circumscribed by the Constitution. As Benjamin Franklin noted, "we have given you a Republic, if you can keep it."

The list of documented coups and bloodbaths undertaken by the Blimp "democrats" since the end of World War II includes Iran, Guatemala, Indonesia, Pakistan, Viet Nam, Brazil, the Balkans, Georgia, the Philippines, Panama, Egypt, Iraq, Libya, Malaysia, most of Central and South America, and, most recently, Syria, Ukraine, and Yemen. Yemen right now is getting the full treatment: horrific genocide, ruthless austerity, and bombing of the country back to the most primitive state of society. The entire continent of Africa has been the scene of similar genocidal warfare and raw materials looting, with child soldiers impressed into the killing. The economies of Mexico, Central America, and most of South America have been turned into outsourced and isolated cheap-labor manufacturing villages sur-

rounded by the production and transportation infrastructure for drugs—the profits from which fuel the Ponzi scheme otherwise known as Wall Street and the City of London.

Numerous political leaders have been assassinated. The Blimps claim credit for some and deny others. The list includes Patrice Lumumba, Aldo Moro, Indira Gandhi, Salvador Allende, John F. Kennedy, Robert Kennedy, Martin Luther King, and Malcolm X. They have murdered pro-development bankers, such as Germany's Alfred Herrhausen, who openly challenged the zero growth and austerity regimes of the IMF and World Bank, the Blimps' collection agencies.

While "Deep State" may be the moniker *du jour* for this leviathan, Lyndon LaRouche provides a clearer and more precise definition when he calls it the **modern British Empire**.

Trump's Sin

Donald Trump's "offense" is that he came out swinging against ideas which the Blimps had spent every day, since Franklin Roosevelt's death on April 12, 1945, establishing as official American orthodoxy.

Don't believe the phony sympathy and outrage about refugees. The bombs of the Blimps and their sponsored drug and terrorist gangs created the refugee crisis, and the Trump critics were nowhere to be found as thousands died in the Mediterranean or were killed by drug gangs in Central America. Don't believe the Blimps' orchestrated outrage about race. Yes, the Trump campaign pandered to the "southern strategists" of the Republican Party with dog whistles, but those incidents

---

5. Friedrich Schiller, in his essay, *Lycurgus and Solon*, provides history's clearest discussion of the differences between the oligarchical model, employed repeatedly under different guises by the Blimps, and the republican model adopted in our Constitution.

are not of the magnitude claimed. Our cities and surrounding suburbs have been frozen in segregated grids for years. Our inner cities are decayed relics of some former civilization and have been that way for decades. "Race" is simply a "card" in the corrupt and cynical games played by these people, a "card" to be played. Bill Clinton, Barack Obama, and their Democratic Leadership Council—spawned by the Senator of "Benign Neglect" Daniel Patrick Moynihan—are hardly in a position to complain about opportunistic racism.[6] Indeed, on behalf of their zero population growth mandates, the Blimps have killed and culled whole populations for almost a century.

EIRNS/Stuart Lewis

Michael Ledeen calls himself a universal fascist.

British Empire apologist John Maynard Keynes.

No, Donald Trump committed his cardinal sin when he said he was open to negotiating with Russia's Putin, and compared Putin's strong leadership of his country unfavorably to Barack Obama's weaknesses. He compounded that by defending the sovereign nation state system against the globalist vision of world government. He linked economic collapse to the collapse of culture. He declared a war on drugs, albeit without the appropriate emphasis, yet, on the role of the money-laundering Wall Street banks. He also endorsed Glass-Steagall banking separation, which would bring the Blimps' casino economy to a halt. He spoke about advancing science—exploring space again and conquering diseases.

Then, on March 20 and March 21, 2017, Trump committed the gravest offense of all, directly embracing the "American System" of political economy, the economic science which actually built the United States and which the Blimps thought they had completely replaced by their free trade and globalist New World Order. All of this represents a deadly strategic threat to the Blimps.

President Trump inherited a very sick foreign policy apparatus called the "Washington consensus," which

spans both political parties. The strategic objectives are the same—the only differences concern tactics. George Bush favored all-out wars; Obama liked to use "soft power," killer special forces, and bombs.

The "consensus" endorses Samuel Huntington's disastrous "clash of civilizations" thesis, inclusive of the neocon, Israeli "clean break" doctrine for the Middle East. This allies the United States with the actual sponsors of terrorism, the perpetrators of 9/11—British sponsored Wahhabi Saudi and other Gulf State fundamentalists. The Blimps are mired in the "zero-sum" British geopolitical mandates dating from the nineteenth century, from Sir Halford Mackinder's dictum that conquest of Eurasia is the key to controlling the world. In their American Century doctrine, the consensus insists that the Blimps must remain the world hegemon, and will kill everyone and anyone who threatens that status. Michael Ledeen, who calls himself a universal fascist, suitably represents this apparatus.

Trump also inherited the Wall Street-funded and corrupted politicians in both political parties who spout failed British economic ideas, whether those of the British-spawned Milton Friedman or the British Empire's apologist, John Maynard Keynes. The models, although seemingly divergent, end at the same place: Malthusian negative population growth, falling rates of human productivity, and imperial control of populations through culture. These alien monetarist ideas have nothing to do with creating sustained development of the physical economy and development of the productive powers of labor, the preoccupations of Alexander Hamilton, Lyndon LaRouche, and now the Chinese in their great *One Belt, One Road* project.

---

6. Moynihan, the favored sociologist of Richard Nixon's southern strategy, declared that the appropriate policy toward the inner cities was "benign neglect." The Clinton Administration disproportionately incarcerated thousands of young black men and women while enacting laws which effectively ended meaningful federal *habeas* review of criminal cases. Barack Obama? What did he ever do about racial inequality except exhibit himself as some kind of post-racial buppie hipster?

To win, the President must kick over the Blimps' Washington devil's chessboard completely. There is no money to realize an infrastructure program which could actually create jobs and restart the economy under the prevailing banking and budgetary axioms. Moreover, the powder keg which is the Wall Street/London bubble economy could explode at any moment. Glass-Steagall must be in place before that happens. At the same time, the Bush and Obama leftovers, together with London and London's NATO allies, remain on a war course with Russia, and it is the President's suggestions for peace that have made him the chief target of the present McCarthyite hysteria.

If President Trump accepts President Xi Jinping's offer for a deal in which China actually helps create productive jobs in the United States, and the U.S., in turn, focuses its productive energies toward developing the world rather than looting it—while both join in exploring space on behalf of the future of all mankind— then, the devil's chessboard gets kicked over completely. A grand strategy for creating a new human renaissance emerges in its wake.

Neoliberalism Defined

A full taxidermy of the Blimps is well beyond the scope of the present report. LaRouche and his associates have written about them, exposed them, and fought directly against them for decades. Rather, we will concentrate, in the space provided, on giving you a horrible taste, if you will, of the truly rotten ideas constituting "democracy," "individual freedom," "free markets," "civil society," and the "arts," as construed by the Blimps.

If you are one of the decent humans, whose good heart is presently being manipulated through the monster image of this President created for you by the Blimps, we hope this report will stop you in your tracks. We hope you can begin to think clearly about the present situation. On the other side of the coin, if you find yourself endlessly and mechanically making connectos, following George Soros' money in the context of the U.S. political situation, we hope to show you just who this economic and cultural hitman actually is, who he works for, and most important, how to defeat him and his bosses. George Soros, so pilloried by Republicans as the ultimate enemy because of his massive early funding of Obama, actually lives and acts by the dictates of von Hayek, Friedman, and von Mises. These are, of course, the evil, British-spawned economists who are worshipped as geniuses and *wunderkinder* by the Conservative Revolutionists now running the former party of Abraham Lincoln. But, we are getting ahead of ourselves.

The biggest dividing line in this battle is what people think about the fundamental nature of human beings. If you believe we are no better than beasts, unable to discern and express universal and profound truths about man and nature, you are on the side of the Blimps. If, however, you believe that we actually participate in God's creation—that humans, uniquely, unlike animals, can discover universal physical principles and derive technologies from them, thereby increasing our "ecological potential,"—you are the enemy of the Blimps. Having declared yourself human, now, Lyndon LaRouche would say, you have to learn to use your mind like a boxer uses his or her fists.

Our report is in three parts. First, we will sketch the array of forces in action against Donald Trump since approximately June 2016, when he secured the Republican nomination. Not surprisingly, this operation is book-ended by the direct actions of British intelligence and represents the same forces and techniques which have been employed by the Blimps in their other "color revolutions," most recently in Ukraine.

Next, we will use the revelations about the Blimps which were documented in the 1967-1975 period in the United States, and isolate some additional developments in 1981-83, to sketch just what this New World Order, violated by Trump, is, provably, all about. We will deal with the evolution of their post-World War I propaganda and psychological warfare apparatus and its fruition in the fascist movements of Europe. We will sketch their post-World War II "democracy" model, put into place after the death of Franklin Roosevelt and sustained by the same psychological warfare and propaganda operations. We will see how that evolved into the disastrous "post-industrial" and "information" societies, which continue, today, to cannibalize our people and our potential on behalf of the City of London and Wall Street.

Finally, we will present two case studies in the modern form of counterinsurgency operations against nations and individuals deemed hostile to the Blimps: the National Endowment for Democracy (NED) and one of its funders and grantees, George Soros. They work together. Whatever the Russians are accused of doing with respect to our elections is chump change when compared to what the U.S. has done, through

Soros and the NED, in engineering *regime change* in country after country throughout the world, all in the name of "free" elections. If someone is elected whom the Blimps have not supported, they are summarily overthrown in a "color revolution" by the NED. Soros has functioned, in most respects, simply as a glorified bagman in these operations.

The techniques employed in those "revolutions," the cartoonish evil monster-image of the target; the use of various color and other symbols to unify a population whose rage has been focused on the target; twenty-four-hour-a-day propaganda incitement by a controlled media; and the complete lack of an actual political program or alternative leadership to that of the target (since succession and program are being arranged in Washington or London), are now on full display against President Trump.

CNN screen capture

CNN spreading propaganda that Russia helped President Trump win the election.

'The Russians Have Landed'—Whoops, It's the British, Once Again

According to the "narrative" provided by the media to the American population, around June 2016, two weeks after Donald Trump was declared the Republican nominee, the Democratic National Committee discovered that its computers had been "hacked." It immediately called in a private company, "CrowdStrike," which declared the source of the attacks to be Russian, particularly Russian state entities.

On July 22, shortly before the Democratic Party convention, Wikileaks published internal Democratic National Committee documents which showed that the DNC was conspiring to destroy the candidacy of Clinton's rival, Bernie Sanders. Barack Obama's DNC Chairman, Debbie Wasserman Shultz, was forced to resign over the ensuing scandal, along with other DNC employees. In October, Wikileaks published emails from John Podesta, Hillary Clinton's campaign manager and the leader of the Center for American Progress, the "idea" factory for the Obama Administration. The Podesta emails elaborated on Hillary Clinton's fawning Wall Street speeches and the scummier financial dealings of the Clinton Foundation. They also showed that Donna Brazile, a commentator for CNN and the then Vice-Chair of the Democratic Party, who is also a creature of the NED, helped Hillary cheat in the CNN-sponsored Presidential debates, by feeding her questions beforehand.

In an obvious attempt to deflect from the damaging proof that Obama and Clinton were, in fact, rigging the election, and had functioned as the corrupt tools of Wall Street and the British, the Clinton campaign played the "Putin demon" black propaganda card. It is important to emphasize that the dangerous propaganda campaign for war with Russia was already in high gear when the Wikileaks documents appeared. Most informed observers believe that if Hillary Clinton had been elected, she would immediately have acted upon her bellicose rhetoric, putting the entire human race at risk in the process. Typical is the *Washington Post* signal opinion piece by the NED's Carl Gershman in October 2016, calling upon the establishment to "summon the will" to overthrow Putin.[7] This war drive began following Obama's coups in Libya and Ukraine, and Putin's responsive interventions in Crimea and Syria.[8]

There are several anomalies lurking beneath the surface in the media's official "narrative" about the alleged Russian hack attack:

---

7. Gershman similarly signaled the impending coup in Ukraine, identifying it as the NED's "biggest prize," in a *Washington Post* article of September 26, 2013.

8. One of the seeming ironies of post-World War II history finds so-called liberal Democrats, led by Barack Obama and Hillary Clinton, engaging, since their Ukraine coup, in a McCarthyite extravaganza targeting Russia and Putin, which rivals that of the infamous Roy Cohn and Senator Joseph McCarthy. Actually, this is not irony at all; the social democrats have simply dropped their pretenses. No longer are we seeing "fascism with a democratic face." We are seeing fascism.

The NED's Carl Gershman called for the overthrow of Russian President Putin in October 2016.

John Podesta, former chairman of the 2016 Hillary Clinton presidential campaign and former counselor to Barack Obama.

1. It has never been established that whatever happened at the DNC or to John Podesta's gmail account had anything to do with the damning Wikileaks releases.

2. CrowdStrike is run by a violently anti-Putin Russian émigré, the Atlantic Council's Dmitri Alperovitch, and one George Kurtz. Kurtz is a personal computer security veteran who founded CrowdStrike as a special project of the long-standing Blimp investment entity known as Warburg Pincus. CrowdStrike has multiple security contracts with U.S. and foreign intelligence agencies. The DNC refused to let the FBI examine the hacked computers and relied solely on CrowdStrike for its forensics and conclusions. The rest of the intelligence community appears to have done the same. Alperovitch alleged, shortly thereafter, that the same hacking gear used by the Russians to hack the DNC had also been used by the Russians to hack various guidance systems of Ukrainian government missiles in Ukraine, a claim that was instantly debunked by almost the entire international computer security community.

3. One of the alleged internal alarms at the DNC that there was something wrong with its computers was the April 2016 report of staffer and consultant Alexandra Chalupa that her computer had been hacked. She was allegedly investigating the ties of then Trump campaign chairman Paul Manafort to Russia and Putin, working with "journalists" and intelligence officials in Ukraine to discredit Manafort and Trump. In other words, she was a Clinton opposition research consultant—in the vernacular an "oppo" operative gathering intelligence against Hillary's rival for the presidency—working with *Ukrainian and other intelligence agencies*, who otherwise collaborate with MI6, the CIA, and with George Soros and the NED's Project Democracy apparatus.

4. Clinton's oppo efforts, massively funded by her PACs, involved collaboration, even at this point, with active or former Anglo-American intelligence agents. The allegations concerning Chalupa's computer were initially used to fuel the bogus media campaign against Manafort, who was then Trump's campaign chairman. Manafort's alleged "sin" was that he, like Tony Podesta, John Podesta's brother, did public relations work for Viktor Yanukovych, the duly elected President of Ukraine, and also lobbied, legally, for some Russian clients. Subsequent media attacks on Manafort, based on never proven "illicit Russian ties," forced his resignation from Trump's campaign. As previously noted, Yanukovych was overthrown in 2014 by Obama, in a color revolution coup which used neo-Nazis as violent "special forces."

5. The FBI and the intelligence community initially didn't buy the Obama/Clinton "oppo" line about Russian interference in the elections and deep Trump ties to Russia. The Director of National Intelligence, James Clapper, for example, stated that he did not know "what all the hyperventilation is about." Clapper alluded to the fact that cyberwar is simply what state intelligence agencies do, the U.S. included. Clapper also knows that the U.S. has intervened to rig elections throughout the world and was probably chary to open that door, absent significant preparation. So, after their initial Putin demon gambit landed with a public thud, and put, ironically, war and peace squarely on the public's agenda, Clinton and Obama produced yet more leaks from anonymous sources. They claimed that election systems in Illinois and Arizona had been hacked by the Russians, and that the Russians were the source of major hacks at media organizations including the *New York Times* and CNN. These stories appeared and disappeared from public view in short order.

According to media accounts, and FBI Director Comey's testimony on March 20, 2017, the FBI opened a counter-intelligence investigation in July 2016, into the Trump campaign's contacts with Russia and Russian "interference" in the election. The media accounts state that it had been abandoned by October for lack of evidence. Comey stated in his March 20 Congressional testimony simply that it had opened in July and continued. A counter-intelligence investigation often involves targeted surveillance and national security wiretaps which cannot be discussed under the law. The penalty for disclosure is ten years in prison. Under Executive Order 12333, governing much of this type of surveillance, officials can lie about its existence in order to protect, "sources and methods."

This lack of official steam, together with candidate Trump's deep skepticism about the whole operation, were entirely warranted. Former NSA whistleblowers and computer security experts contested the claims of Russian hacking. Wikileaks stated that its source for the documents was not Russia, but an insider, a whistleblower. Former U.S. intelligence professionals, including the NSA's William Binney and the CIA's Ray McGovern provided a detailed report supporting Wikileaks' whistle-blower claims. During this period, numerous other computer security analysts pointed to flaws in CrowdStrike's analysis. Among the more interesting were those noting that state security cyberwar typically relies on intercepts, rather than hacks—pointing to the famous Russian recording of the State Department's Victoria Nuland dictating that her "Yats" would replace Yanukovych as Ukraine's leader in a conversation which also included her famous admonition to "fuck the EU."

The biggest and smelliest anomaly in the concocted media narrative, however, is the *Guardian* story of January 7, 2017, and a similar story in the *New York Times*, which noted that British intelligence, specifically GCHQ, "alarmed" about the Trump campaign's "pro-Russian" stance and contacts, tipped off U.S. intelligence that the DNC had been hacked, *back in Autumn of 2015*. If that is true, then Obama and the DNC knew about the alleged hacks months before revealing them and, if you believe their own "narrative," did absolutely nothing about them.

6. In October and November 2017 a new escalation of the Trump/Putin demonization campaign was begun. A dodgy and salacious dossier was circulated from the Obama/Clinton opposition research team, claiming that the President-elect engaged in perverse sexual acts while in Russia, and could be blackmailed by Putin as a result. The dossier amplified public statements by candidate Clinton and a Washington, D.C. whisper campaign to the effect that Donald Trump was a "Manchurian candidate," a Putin puppet. By October 29, Harry Reid had already gone before Congress to declare that the FBI was withholding devastating information about the Trump campaign's ties to Russia, and that he had received classified briefings about the matter. The dodgy dossier also provided numerous allegations to back up the phony Russian election "interference" claims, as well as providing new claims about Manafort's alleged Russian ties. The dodgy dossier had so little credibility that most media outlets, who otherwise bit on every hysterical morsel fed to them about Trump, refused to publish it.

7. But then, in January, *Buzzfeed*, which had frequently published raw Clinton/Obama "oppo" stories, published the fake dodgy dossier in full. The U.S. intelligence community, particularly Obama's ghoulish grand inquisitor, CIA head John Brennan, proceeded to give it credibility by leaking that both President-elect Trump and President Obama had been briefed on its contents.

The author of the dodgy dossier was Christopher Steele, a "former" British intelligence agent who, the *Guardian* reported, once headed the Russian desk of MI6, and now was on contract to the Clinton oppo team. Thus, the effort to delegitimize the Trump Presidency emanated from the highest levels of Anglo-American intelligence—the authors of endless coups and political assassinations. It was accompanied by a "unanimous" but factless public "official assessment" by the U.S. intelligence community (reportedly dragging both the FBI and the NSA reluctantly along). It "assessed" that Putin had personally directed a hacking campaign to interfere with the election and tip it in Trump's favor. Rather than provide facts to back this "assessment," the appendix to the official report is an attack on Russian press outlets, particularly *RT* (rt.com), for successful "propaganda" efforts in the United States. As we shall see, this targeting, which seemed so McCarthyite and plainly weird at the time, was hardly accidental.

The Democrats, the news media, and Blimp Republicans, led by McCain and Graham, went berserk, demanding special prosecutors and Congressional investigations, and sneering that "other shoes" were about to drop. Democratic Senator Mark Warner, his voice shaking, and looking in every respect like the overgrown adolescent that he is, solemnly declared that investigating and pumping these allegations was the most important moment of his life. Other Democrats and allied media, like the *New York Times'* Thomas Friedman, having clearly lost it, claimed that Russia had committed an "act of war," presumably seeking to invoke Article 5 of the NATO treaty.

8. On March 1, 2017, the *New York Times* revealed that Obama and his national security colleagues had spent the months after the election dropping a trail of "leads" in official documents, and leaking information in the effort to destroy Trump and to continue their policies against Russia and China.

Obama's Director of National Intelligence, James Clapper.

There were two publicly known and extremely significant Obama Administration actions in this process. On December 24, 2016, Obama signed the National Defense Authorization Act, which includes the "Countering Foreign Propaganda and Disinformation Act." It aims to mobilize the entire government, U.S. media, academia, NGOs, and foreign partners and allies to "expose and counter" foreign propaganda and disinformation directed against U.S. national security interests and "proactively advance fact-based narratives that support United States allies and interests." The primary target for this black propaganda, fake news offensive is the population of the United States. During the Reagan Administration, such activities were called Active Measures and, at least legally, confined to foreign targets.

The NDAA's incredible Orwellian assault on the First Amendment was preceded by a November 25, 2016 *Washington Post* story publishing the names of several media outlets, which it labeled Russian propaganda fronts. The list of media outlets smeared as Russian agents was provided by an anonymous group tied to the government and calling themselves "Prop or Not." The list included not only *RT* and *Sputnik*, but also *Consortium News, Breitbart,* the *Drudge Report, Truthout* and other "left" critics of Obama, *AntiWar. com,* and the *Ron Paul Institute.* In short, just about everyone who had criticized the Obama/Clinton war drive against Russia.[9] Facebook and other social media out-

lets immediately launched initiatives to censor and curtail "fake news."

Obama complained bitterly throughout the election campaign that Americans had displayed a disturbing propensity to believe the Russians, rather than Obama, on issues of war and peace. This is hardly a shocking development based on repeated and demonstrable lies by his and like American administrations concerning the war in Viet Nam, 9/11, the war in Iraq, the war in Syria, the coup in Ukraine, the coup and assassination of Qadaffi in Libya, the terrorist assault on Benghazi, the mass surveillance state exposed by Edward Snowden, etc. Based on Obama's bizarre public comments, it appears that he already knew that his administration's active measures program, described by Cass Sunstein as "cognitively infiltrating" the brains of domestic opponents, was simply not working.[10]

Then, on December 15, 2016, DNI James Clapper signed new procedures allowing the NSA to distribute raw intercept data throughout the entire intelligence community. These procedures became official on January 3, 2017 when Attorney General Loretta Lynch signed off on them. The revision had been in the works for over a year. At issue is modification of secret procedures under E.O. 12333, deemed by Edward Snowden and others as the most significant authority for our present, completely unconstitutional, surveillance state. Previously, the NSA was required to filter and redact information regarding U.S. citizens monitored in for-

---

9. We have been told by a source that the only reason LaRouche was not on this public list was that entities associated with him had long been subject to active measures under E.O. 12333 by both Bush and Obama.

10. See Tony Papert, "Obama Aide Sunstein Outlines Plan to Suppress Opposition," *EIR*, May 16, 2012.

eign counterintelligence activities. Thus, officials who have been leaking raw intercept data about Trump to the national news media could claim some degree of immunity from prosecution under the combined legal impact of the NDAA and the revised E.O. 12333. Moreover, any search for leakers became infinitely more difficult.

The *New York Times* and other outlets have constantly referred to leaked intercepts or FISA warrants over the course of their demonization campaign against Trump. In some cases, the claims involved two alleged applications to the FISA court about Trump and his associates, one of them turned down, the other resulting in a surveillance order in October. The FBI, through the Justice Department's National Security Division, makes these secret requests pursuant to counterintelligence and terrorism investigations. The first, right after the DNC hacking allegations emerged, was allegedly too broad even for the FISA Court, which seldom turns down applications. That application, if it exists, could prove significant in showing the sources and intentions of the conspirators against Trump. The October warrant application was reportedly narrowed to a server which allegedly was tied to allegations concerning the Trump campaign's contacts with two Russian banks. Other leaks simply refer to intercepts.

Most experts on the matter, including former NSA executive William Binney, former Ambassador Jack Matlock, and Colin Powell's former chief of staff, Colonel Lawrence Wilkerson, agree that the most likely source of these leaks is raw NSA intercepts generated under E.O. 12333 or intercepts by GCHQ, the NSA's British counterpart, which functions under E.O. 12333 without any of the constraints of U.S. law. GCHQ monitors the entire world's communications channels through the cables on which they pass under the Atlantic. The British press reports that the head of GCHQ appears to have been mysteriously fired right in the midst of the Trump-Russia contretemps. Adding another piece to the puzzle, Wikileaks recently released the CIA's hacking tool-chest which includes the ability to run "false-flag" operations. In other words, the CIA, MI6, and allied intelligence agencies have the ability to hack and leave a trail ascribing the hacks to other governments, such as Russia.

9. On March 4, 2017, the President interrupted the entire fake media narrative by tweeting that Obama had him "wiretapped" in Trump Tower prior to the election and that what was happening to him reeked of McCarthyism. The media, which had been publishing allegations about FISA warrants and intercepts of Trump or his associates for months, erupted in what has to be one the largest and most shameless demonstrations of the Big Lie ever known. They declared that Trump was offering wild claims with no evidence, essentially circling back on their very own reporting and labeling it, "fake news."

As has been the case throughout the media's war on Trump, the Tweet was deconstructed to its most literal and bizarre potential meaning. The media focused on the literal term "wiretapped," declaring that the President was off his rocker and making unsubstantiated claims to the American public. By the media's bizarre rendition, the President meant that Barack Obama himself surreptitiously entered Trump Tower and placed a physical tap on Trump's phones. Other efforts to discredit the President's claim, including statements by various intelligence officials and hostile Congressmen, are constructed around the literal interpretation that Trump himself, personally, was wiretapped rather than individuals or entities associated with him. In all of it, Trump's truthful claim, that his presidential campaign and its associates were surveilled by the Obama Administration and that he is a victim of McCarthyism, gets deliberately lost in the daily news cycle.

Americans should remember that the intelligence community swore up and down, under oath, in testimony to Congress that there was no mass surveillance of the American population. Edward Snowden's disclosures proved that claim, made under penalties of perjury, to be an out and out lie. Another fact lost in the blizzard of "commentary" is the consistent finding of the intelligence community that in all of their investigations, under whatever rubric they were conducted, they found absolutely no collusion whatsoever between the Trump campaign and Russia.

It is very unlikely that FBI Director Comey's March 20, 2017 politically motivated revelation that the FBI counterintelligence investigation launched in July of 2016 is continuing, will change that fact. Comey had already briefed Congressional leaders about the results of that investigation up to the time of his testimony. Those briefings resulted in Congressional leaders stating there was no collusion between the Trump campaign and Russia. The sole holdouts are Democrats, led by California Congressman Adam Schiff, who is now trying on the Joe McCarthy tin-foil hat before the TV

C-Span

James Comey, Jr., Director of the FBI.

C-Span

Without evidence, California Democratic Congressman Adam Schiff maintains that there was collusion between Russia and the Trump campaign.

cameras. Schiff looks every bit like a cross between Charlie Brown and a Conehead, with the grasping and crazy personality of Lucy Van Pelt. As a prosecutor, it took him three tries to convict the hapless former FBI agent Richard Miller of espionage, despite overwhelming and salacious evidence. In his statement at the House Intelligence Committee on March 20, he wove a tortured conspiracy theory relying for factual content exclusively on the British dodgy dossier. Schiff's conspiracy theory was immediately labeled the Democrats' "best case" by a fawning media.

10. Press Secretary Sean Spicer escalated the battle on March 16, 2017 by quoting a Fox News personality, Judge Andrew Napolitano, accurately pointing to Britain's GCHQ as a major player in the attacks on the President. The Blimps collectively went wild over a direct attack directed at the appropriate target. As is often noted in investigations, guilt spills itself for fear of being spilt.

In other words, we are witnessing a very elaborate and dangerous British hoax which gambles the very future of our nation. The actual crimes, the violations of the law in leaking raw intercepts without redaction, the targeting of a political opponent by the Obama Administration (intelligence agencies have been trained for decades to provide deniability for the President in all of these operations), and the open collaboration of intelligence agencies with the Clinton presidential campaign, are intended to be covered up and forever hidden. The essential target of this campaign—the potential for an alliance with China, Russia, and Japan to develop the world—will, it is hoped, be wiped out forever.

Meanwhile, the mega-donor funders for Clinton and Obama, the participants with George Soros in the Democracy Alliance of billionaires, have taken their war against Trump to the streets. With the imaginations of gnats (remember they believe that the population's deepest hopes and desires are nothing but algorithms to be exploited), they declared that they would re-enact the Tea Party movement, this time against Trump. An amalgam of parochial and "identity politics" special interests—gays, suburban professional women, Hollywood entertainment figures, upwardly mobile minorities, environmentalists, and the professional class of lawyers, accountants, journalists, and techies—now constitutes the Democratic Party's base.[11] The working class and farmers have been dumped entirely. This amalgam is now mobilized under the simple color revolution slogan, "resist." Michael Moore has sallied forth to incite the more Jacobin and anarchist elements of this base. He incites by instructing that the duly elected President of the United States is to be treated like a "pedophile."

Since Obama's election in 2008, a parallel structure built from that election has dominated Democratic politics. State chairs and traditional Democratic Party constituency leaders were largely ignored. The "working class" was abandoned in favor of an army of professionals and the entitled, all wrapped in the Hollywood glitz and glamor essential to Barack Obama's endless

---

11. Both Thomas Frank, in his book, *Listen Liberal* (Picador, New York, 2016), and Christopher Lasch in his last book, *Revolt of the Elites* (W.W. Norton, New York, 1995), describe this mix of the elite and the entitled as the fatal, final blow to the party of Franklin Roosevelt. Trump advisor Steve Bannon has described Lasch's work as one of his favorite books.

preening of himself. Significant funding was put into training professional organizers for Organizing for Action, Move On, the Working Families Party, and other entities, by the billionaires of the Democracy Alliance, which includes George Soros as only one of its billionaire donors.

The programs for both Obama's presidency and this artificial "movement" were produced out of John Podesta's Center for American Progress. Permanent organizations operating under this flag have existed since 2008 on both coasts, dot the "swing states" and electoral college map, and have even expanded into traditional red-state areas like Texas, where all-out efforts were made in 2014 to exploit the "Hispanic demographic" which, it was claimed, would produce Democratic victories in the state.

This Obama/Democratic Leadership Council formation has left the Democratic Party in the worst shape in its entire historical existence. It has lost the Presidency, both houses of Congress, and almost every governorship in the United States. At the donors' meetings which led to the present "resist" mobilization, it is reliably reported that the donors—fearing a complete split by Sanders supporters, who wanted real change and had been repeatedly kicked in the face by the "Democrats in Name Only" Obama apparatus—settled on the "resist" color-revolution strategy as a matter of pure survival. They have absolutely no positive program.

The Democracy Alliance trained its present street cadre in the "community control" and parochial incitement methods of Saul Alinsky, who also trained both Barack Obama and Hillary Clinton. In recent years, Alinsky's tactics have been supplemented with the psychological warfare techniques employed in various color revolutions. The demonstrations now sweeping the country are orchestrated by these people, exploiting genuine fears created by the monster image of Donald Trump elaborated every minute of the day by the nation's media. The President is portrayed as "murderer" Putin's crony, plunderer of women, killer of the dreams of immigrants and the vulnerable, authoritarian dictator to be—a rage-provoking cartoon addressed to the labile, the volatile, and the credulous.

The scene is truly like falling through the rabbithole into Alice in Wonderland. Now, the otherwise imperiled and ideologically bankrupt Democratic Party leadership mans the barricades. A huge women's march preceded the inauguration, featuring thousands of women in pink pussy-cat hats, allegedly protesting the

CC/Mobilus In Mobili

Mega-donor funders for Hillary Clinton and Obama have taken their war against Trump to the streets. One example is the Jan. 21, 2017 Women's March on Washington, shown here.

President's pro-life stance and "locker room" talk about pussy grabbing. Many participants were shocked as they found themselves enveloped in a variety of left-radical causes *du jour*, about which they know next to nothing.[12] The very dirty Chuck Schumer and the doddering Nancy Pelosi daily incite the mob through an ever-receptive media who hang on their every word. Democratic women, hardly vestal virgins, showed up dressed all in white for the President's address to Congress. The former Attorney General of the United States, Loretta Lynch, in a video posted to the website of the Democratic Senatorial Committee, invoked Selma and Bloody Sunday, and urged people to take the streets. The *Washington Post*, a Blimp house organ of the first order,[13] appears with the creepy subhead in its logo, "Democracy Dies in Darkness."

12. Gloria Steinem, the founder of modern feminism, herself labored in the *Kulturkampf* for the CIA in the 1960s as a student. She states that she is very proud of that service. But, again, we are ahead of ourselves.

13. In 1976, the *Washington Post*'s CIA associated editorial page editor, Stephen Rosenfeld, published an op-ed instructing journalists throughout the country not to cover Lyndon LaRouche at all. Or, if he was covered, he must be presented in the most negative way possible. Those orders were strictly followed.

As Trump rightly insists, all of the theater we are witnessing has nothing to do with why Hillary Clinton lost the election. Hillary Clinton sealed her fate by calling Trump voters a racist, misogynist "batch of deplorables." She adamantly refused to address the economic depression prevalent everywhere except in the enclaves of the professional and elite classes on the nation's coasts, sticking to the demographic data computer-scenarios utilized by Obama. She campaigned against Glass-Steagall and tied herself completely to Barack Obama's failed legacy. Clinton's criminal idiocy was echoed by Barack Obama himself, who speechified about how he created an economic recovery—a declaration made as the U.S. death rate soared among boomers and gen-xers, as most formerly industrial states battled a drug and suicide epidemic, and as whole sections of his own former organizing turf in Chicago exploded in drug and gang related murders.[14] There is only so long you can spit in peoples' faces and call it rain.

LaRouche PAC organizers have found an open receptivity among the demonstrators, once the point is driven home that "resist" has absolutely no agenda for creating a productive economy, and that the issue driving the entire matter is the Blimps' intention for a third world war. As Martin Luther King so eloquently noted, economic and social progress are the true measures of any society—the true mandate of Heaven.

II. Waking Up in Wonderland— The Revelations of 1968-1975: Fake News, Fake Culture

Lyndon LaRouche recounts that when he returned from World War II, he, like other veterans who fought heroically to vanquish fascism, suddenly found themselves in a mass-culture reeking of banality and conformity. "Get ahead. Make money. Don't think big ideas—you'll get in trouble." Roosevelt's optimistic sense of national purpose and the accompanying appetite for great deeds, big ideas, grand projects, and exploring the frontiers of science and the human mind, seemed,

somehow, to be under massive, sustained assault, the full scope of which would only become clear many years later.

Some in the baby-boomer generation got a further glimpse into this process when they awoke, as young adults, to find that what they thought were their precious individual free thoughts, and what they thought were their "free" individual "choices"—those "modern" and avant-garde preferences for certain novels, movies, or music—had been manufactured for them by a bunch of bought and paid-for academics and artists working for Wall Street, the City of London, and their associated intelligence agencies.

In 1966-1967, *Ramparts Magazine* and the *New York Times* revealed that the Congress for Cultural Freedom (CCF)—an institution of influential academics, writers, and musicians, including many people in the extremely significant New York City intelligentsia—were being funded by the CIA to shape and control public opinion both in the United States and abroad, nominally as part of the Cold War against the Soviet Union.

An uncontrolled culture and intelligentsia, it was argued, was a fertile ground for Communism, or the equally evil nationalism and neutralism, in the geopolitical battle being waged by the Anglo-Americans to control the world. According to Frances Stoner Saunders' definitive history of the CCF,[15] there is not a musician or artist from this entire period who was not influenced in some way by this operation.

Then, in 1971, a band of anti-war activists broke into the FBI offices in Media, Pennsylvania, purloining reams of FBI files. Some of these files bore the mysterious heading, "COINTELPRO," or counterintelligence program. Shocking revelations of domestic political actions by the FBI and CIA designed to disrupt and control the emergent civil rights and anti-War movements followed, culminating in the Watergate scandal and the resignation of President Richard M. Nixon.

Through media exposés and Congressional hearings, Americans learned that the CIA and FBI had com-

---

14. *EIR* detailed the dismal results of "community control" and similar Alinskyite organizing in 1979, citing a series by reporter Roy Harvey showing how a Field Foundation operation in Chicago exploded in violence by the gangs being manipulated in a human social experiment. "The Gangs—Who Benefits," *EIR*, April 7, 1979. The same gang/drug gang violence is responsible for Chicago's horrendous murder rate today.

15. Saunders, *The Cultural Cold War*, The New Press, New York, 2000. Among the writers who worked with CCF not otherwise referenced in this report, were Robert Lowell, Mary McCarthy, Allen Tate, John Crowe Ransom, Diane Trilling, and Alfred Kazin. The fascist poets, Ezra Pound and T.S. Elliot, were separately groomed by the CIA's J.J. Angleton. Literary critics and social scientists included Edmund Wilson, Edward Shils, Elizabeth Hardwick, Norman Podhoretz, and Susan Sontag.

More than one hundred people participated in the founding of the Congress for Cultural Freedom, in West Berlin, June 1950.

pletely penetrated the trade unions in the United States and that the AFL-CIO's international division, led by ex-Communist Jay Lovestone, a J.J. Angleton CIA operative, was a completely controlled intelligence entity. The revelations included J. Edgar Hoover's infamous effort to induce Martin Luther King to commit suicide; murderous gang wars instigated by U.S. intelligence against the Black Panther Party; and other informant, provocateur, and financial warfare operations designed to destroy insurgent political organizations and psychologically shred their leaders. The FBI and CIA engaged in endless black bag burglaries, mail openings, and illegal electronic surveillance (the NSA's "Operation Minaret") to build salacious dossiers on every major political figure in the United States, wielding them, when appropriate, for blackmail purposes.

The CIA had also widely experimented with mass brainwashing techniques, including the use of psychotropic drugs for this purpose. After the Viet Nam War, it was also revealed that drugs from the Golden Triangle had been a major financing source for U.S. covert operations throughout Southeast Asia.

In the world at large, the United States with its British master, were revealed to be the masterminds of coups and myriad assassinations against any nation or leader not slavishly devoted to the Blimps. Nations which proclaimed themselves neutral or nationalist were targeted for coups and assassinations. Intellectuals who refused to join the anti-Red hysteria suddenly found themselves ostracized, broke, and alone.

The national news media of both Britain and the United States were exposed as active collaborators in

these operations. In his groundbreaking 1977 *Rolling Stone* piece, Carl Bernstein cites more than 400 prominent journalists as CIA tainted, either as actual agents operating under journalistic cover, or as directly collaborating in Agency propaganda operations. While every major news outlet was implicated, the *New York Times*, *Readers Digest*, Henry Luce's *Time-Life*, and CBS News, played the most significant roles. Bernstein emphasized that his count did not include the large stable of journalists who worked for the evil James J. Angleton, a British agent within the CIA. He noted that while these operations were a known fact, Angleton was meticulous in not creating a record.

The other major players in what the CIA's Frank Wisner called the "Mighty Wurlitzer" orchestration of public opinion, were the Wall Street-centered foundations, most prominently the Ford and Rockefeller Foundations, with which the CIA worked on many joint social experiments, very often sharing or switching funding back and forth. The CIA also ran foundations of its own, the most famous being the Fairfield Foundation which laundered CIA funds going to the CCF.

In Britain, the same investigations exposed the allied and infamous Information Research Department. The IRD involved journalists, editors, professors, scientists, and labor leaders working with MI5 and MI6 in counterinsurgency and propaganda operations targeting the populations of Britain and Western Europe, Africa, and Asia, generally, and the intelligentsia specifically.

World War I and the 'Hitler Project'

This public opinion and social control apparatus had its first U.S. incarnation in the racist Woodrow Wilson Administration following World War I.[16] It is firmly

---

16. As *EIR* has documented, Wilson presided over the resurrection and glorification of the Ku Klux Klan from the White House and was controlled by British agent Edward House. See D. Speed, "Jim Crow, a Cultural Weapon in the Hands of the Confederacy," *EIR*, April 15, 1994.

Walter Lippmann

rooted in the counterinsurgency methods of British colonialism. Harold Laswell and Walter Lippmann pioneered the conscious applications of these methods in the United States by building a social science army which experimented, profiled, and polled human populations while mastering propaganda techniques in order, in Lippmann's words, to "manufacture" popular democratic consent.

Lippmann spent World War I at the British psychological warfare and propaganda headquarters in Wellington House, outside of London, in a group that included Sigmund Freud's nephew, Eduard Bernays.[17] In his book, *Public Opinion*, Lippman writes that it is through media, particularly modern mass communications like movies, that most people come to develop the "pictures in their heads" of themselves, of others, of their needs and purposes, and their relationships. He observes that people are more than willing to reduce complex problems to simplistic formulas, to form their opinion by what they believe others around them believe: Truth hardly enters into such considerations. Appearance of reports in the media confer the aura of reality upon those stories: If they weren't factual, the average person believes, then why would they be reported?

People whose fame is built up by the media, such as movie stars, Lippmann argued, can become "opinion leaders," with as much power to sway public opinion as

political figures. He marveled at the power of movies. Words, or even a still picture, require an effort by a person to form a "picture in the mind." But, with a movie, "the whole process of observing, describing, reporting, and then imagining is accomplished for you. Without much more trouble than is needed to stay awake, the result which your imagination is always aiming at is reeled off the screen." Significantly, he cites D.W. Griffith's propaganda film for the Ku Klux Klan, *The Birth of a Nation*, writing that no American will ever hear the name of the Klan again, "without seeing those white horsemen."[18]

Popular opinion, Lippman writes, must ultimately be determined by the desires and wishes of an elite, rich, and superior social set, fundamentally international in scope, whose center is in London. But, the use of this instrument requires precision. "Public opinion must be organized for the press, not by the press." The organizers must be a "specialized class" which operates through "intelligence bureaus."

Similarly, Harold Laswell, who reviewed all propaganda efforts conducted by the state parties to World War I for his doctoral thesis, and was fascinated by the application of Freudian psychology to mass population control, wrote:

"The spread of literacy did not release the masses from ignorance and superstition but altered the nature of both and compelled the development of whole new techniques of control, largely through propaganda… [A propagandist's] regard for men rests on no democratic dogmatisms about men being the best judges of their own interests. The modern propagandist, like the modern psychologist, recognizes that men are poor judges of their own interest… [Those with power must cultivate] sensitiveness to those concentrations of motive which are implicit and available for rapid mobilizations when the appropriate symbol is offered… [The propagandist is] no phrasemonger but a promoter of overt acts."[19]

Lippman founded the *New Republic* magazine, deliberately modeled after the "Open Conspiracy" nostrums of H.G. Wells, and is considered to be the founder

---

17. Bernays was extremely important in his own right. He pioneered methods of popular consent in mass marketing through advertising and went on to work for the CIA in such propaganda efforts as the Dulles/United Fruit coup in Guatemala.

18. See L. Wolfe, "How the British Use the Media For Mass Psychological Warfare," *EIR*, January 17, 1997.
19. Quoted in Christopher Simpson, *The Science of Coercion, Communication Research and Psychological Warfare 1945-1960*, Oxford University Press, New York, 1994.

of modern journalism and communications theory.[20] The U.S. studies in mass psychological manipulation in the inter-war period were almost entirely funded by the Rockefeller Foundation, although not without some opposition. Donald Slesinger, former dean of the University of Chicago, described its ideas as using a democratic "guise" to "tacitly accept the objectives and methods of a new form of authoritarianism... We have thought about fighting dictatorships by force through the establishment of dictatorship by manipulation," he said. Joseph Willits, a Rockefeller officer, described these ideas as frankly "fascist."[21]

These propaganda and social control techniques were further "weaponized" by both Anglo-American psychological warfare techniques utilized in World War II, and the fascist revolutions led by Hitler and Mussolini, but produced by Wall Street, London, and very old European oligarchic networks.

Helga Zepp-LaRouche, in her groundbreaking study, *The Hitler Book*, thoroughly explores the Anglo-American and oligarchic roots of the German fascist phenomena. As she relates, the German economy was reduced to devastation by the terms of the Versailles Treaty. John Maynard Keynes, who negotiated the Versailles conditions, referred to the impossible reparations demands made on Germany as an experiment in "white slavery." At the same time, a witches' brew of synthetic belief structures was concocted through the mystical and racist Thule Society, the Anglo-American sponsored eugenics movement, the geopolitical theories of Mackinder and Karl Haushofer, and the synarchist Pan-European movement of Count Richard Cou-

In 1923 and 1943, Time *magazine featured Mussolini on its cover, and referred to him in articles as "Wonderful Benito."*

denhove-Kalergi. The insane "philosopher" Friedrich Nietzsche is a marker for the extreme, irrational pessimism fostered in the post- World War I German population under conditions of economic slavery.

The Conservative Revolution ideology ultimately embraced by Hitler was only one of several competing Nazi-Communist synthetic movements in the post-war period. Hitler won that competition over the national bolshevist "left" socialist current led by Georg Strasser. Neither would have been possible without the cultural murder of the spirit emanating from the Liberation Wars against Napoleon, and the German "classic" culture which accompanied them. The Congress of Vienna, the Carlsbad decrees, and the routing of Otto Bismarck, were all designed to kill the nascent German republican movement.

In Italy, a Venetian oligarchical group led by Count Piero Foscari and including Count Giuseppe Volpi di Misurata, Count Vittorio Cini, and many of the families constituting the former Venetian Council, sponsored and ran the Mussolini project. Mussolini's controller was Volpi di Misurata, who was an open British agent. Volpi also coordinated U.S. and British financial support for the project with Montagu Norman. His color revolution began in 1922 when gangs of black-shirted thugs descended on Rome. The various propaganda themes utilized by Il Duce drew on the myth-making of Georges Sorel and Gabriele d'Annunzio, to sell the imperial model of Rome to a population hungry for relief from financial despair and the paralysis of government. The elites would protect the "little man" and lead him to glory.

As the LaRouche movement has repeatedly documented, the British elite and their American satraps on Wall Street, spent the 20s and early 30s building up fascist movements in Italy, Germany, Spain, and the United States. Of particular note were the actions of the Morgan, Harriman, and Du Pont interests. In 1926, for

20. Lippmann, who migrated from the British Fabian Society to the circles of Thomas Dewey and the Dulles Brothers, became the spokesman for the British-controlled American imperialist faction, deployed against the anti-imperialist polices of FDR. See Lyndon LaRouche, *The Case of Walter Lippmann* (New York, Campaigner Publications, 1977).
21. Simpson, op. cit., p. 23.

example, Morgan partner Thomas Lamont arranged a $100 million loan to Mussolini's government. Henry Luce's *Time*, *Life*, and *Fortune* magazines repeatedly lauded Mussolini, featuring him on *Time*'s covers in 1923 and 1943, while articles in *Time* called him "Wonderful Benito!"

Numerous books have been written about the Anglo-American sponsorship of the Nazi regime.[22] John Foster Dulles, as a lawyer for the Morgans and the Rockefellers, patronized Hjalmar Schacht and the Thyssen industrial cartel until the mid-1940s. Prescott Bush, the scion of the Bush family, helped finance the Thyssen cartel through Union Bank, an instrument of Brown Brothers Harriman, got caught, and was outed under the

Nazi Propaganda Minister Joseph Goebbels said he used British methods.

Trading with the Enemy Act. The Harrimans sponsored Ernst Rudin, the Nazis' race theorist, in lectures to their Eugenics Society here in the United States. The Bank of England's Montagu Norman and Hjalmar Schacht were essential instruments in Hitler's ascension to power and in the building of the Nazi war machine.

With what we now know about this sponsorship, it is difficult not to conclude that the touted propaganda campaigns of Joseph Goebbels and Hitler himself had an Anglo-American sponsorship. Leni Riefenstahl's widely acclaimed movie *Triumph of the Will*, for example, presents Hitler as the ultimate kindly environmentalist. Goebbels claimed to be following British methods in scientific exploitation of propaganda in the Nazi state, and conducted polling and other studies in pursuit of his objective. Sefton Delmer, Lord Beaverbrook's agent to the Nazis, was the only journalist Hitler allowed to travel with him prior to the outbreak of war. Delmer would go on to lead Britain's black pro-

paganda operations in World War II.

The oligarchy's fascist experiment blew up when their Frankenstein attacked England itself.

The Roosevelt Issue

Franklin Roosevelt was elected on an explicitly anti-Wall Street platform. He openly declared Wall Street's hatred of him to be his political badge of honor. He defeated their attempted coups and assassinations—run through such entities as the fascist Liberty League—by engaging and educating the "silent majority," spending hours and hours preparing his thoroughly composed radio addresses to the people. He knew, instinctively, what the studies of Wall Street's social scientists also revealed: An actual human identity is awakened when large segments of the population are engaged in a growing productive economy, advancing the frontiers of scientific, artistic, and industrial knowledge. As is clear from the writings of Lasswell and Lippmann, the Blimps' "democratic" Malthusian regimes rely upon the opposite—a thoroughly stupefied and docile population.

Roosevelt's allies in the American intelligence community had the Anglo-American Hitler project under a microscope, prior to World War II. U.S. government archives, made available to *EIR*, feature extensive intelligence reports on the international fascist plots from the files of the State Department, Army and Navy Intelligence, the Coordinator of Information, and its successor, the Office of Strategic Services (OSS). The files feature the subject header: "Synarchist/Nazi-Communist." In 1947, OSS veteran and Harvard professor William L. Langer detailed the Roosevelt Administration's dealings with Vichy France, noting the reactionary movement known as the Synarchy. It had been in existence for nearly a century.[23] Its aim had always been to

---

22. For a comprehensive account of Hitler's Anglo-American origins see Helga Zepp-LaRouche, *The Hitler Book*, Schiller Institute, New York, 1984. See also Antony Sutton's *Wall Street and the Rise of Hitler*, Charles Higham's *Trading With the Enemy*, James Stewart Martin's *All Honorable Men*, David Talbot's *Devil's Chessboard: Allen Dulles, the CIA and the Rise of America's Secret Government*.

23. Langer, *Our Vichy Gamble*, New York, A.A. Knopf, 1947, pp. 167-170.

Wikipedia

Carl Schmitt

Wikipedia

Leo Strauss

Wikipedia

Martin Heidegger

Kurt Lewin

dent, depression followed, and the "American Century"[24] paradigm was instituted.

In pursuing a separate peace with the Nazis, Allen Dulles, John J. McCloy, and William Draper conducted what is perhaps history's ultimate cover-up. Under their operation, leading Nazis were never prosecuted, but were assimilated, instead, into the post-War "Gladio" networks of NATO, into Anglo-American intelligence, and into their controlled intelligentsia. Carl Schmitt, the author and philosopher of the Nazis' legal system, and Martin Heidegger, one of its most influential philosophers, became protected intellectual assets. Schmitt arranged with the Rockefeller Foundation for the emigration of his admirer, Leo Strauss, to London and the United States. Strauss was a devotee of Schmitt, Heidegger, and Alexandre Kojève, who preached the doctrine of "purgative violence" as a necessary state in the evolution of individuals. Using a perverse methodology, Strauss created a neoconservative cult consisting of selected students of his at the University of Chicago, a cult largely responsible for the Iraq War.[25]

Schacht, Hitler's paymaster, was prosecuted at Nuremberg but escaped punishment by threatening to expose the bankers' cartel behind the Hitler project. The biographies of the oligarchical authors of the European fascist project were subjected to public relations scrubs and history was rewritten, allowing for the launch of a renewed geopolitical project for establishing a globalist "world" empire, this time through "terror of nuclear weapons."[26] Under that rubric, two competing empires would be allowed to dominate the world, that of the Soviet Union and that of

carry out a bloodless revolution, inspired by the upper classes, aimed at producing a form of government by technicians, under which domestic and foreign policy would be subordinated to international banking and financial interests.

At the end of the war, Franklin Roosevelt declared that he would put an end to the British Empire. He envisioned worldwide economic development, based upon the mutual self-interests of nation states, as the post-war model for the world, an arrangement which would foster continued economic growth. When he died, Wall Street moved quickly to reinstate its oligarchic imperial model, this time in a more developed, fake-democratic form. Harry Truman became Presi-

---

24. Characterized by LaRouche and others as the use of "British brains"—to wit, imperial grand strategy—employing "American brawn" to achieve its objectives.

25. LaRouche PAC's *Children of Satan* provides a history of this process as viewed through the prism of the creation of the war on Iraq, a monstrous, murderous exercise conducted for imperial reasons based on systemic official and media lies to the population.

26. Initially, in the Oct. 1, 1946 issue of the *Bulletin of the Atomic Scientists*, Bertrand Russell advocated a preemptive nuclear strike on the Soviet Union.

the Anglo-Americans, in existential and deadly competition with one another in a "Cold War." The American System, the ideas of the American revolution, and the efforts to spread and institutionalize these ideas in Europe and Russia, were to be thoroughly erased in the process.

The central idea-factories in this drive were the post-war British Tavistock Institute, including psychologist Kurt Lewin and his colleagues in the United States, the anti-Communist "left" intellectuals and social democrats of the CCF, the Frankfurt School of nihilist German intellectuals, and the conservative and libertarian "thinkers" of the Mont Pelerin Society.

Bertrand Russell, one of five honorary chairman of the CCF.

The Post-War New World Order

The writings of Bertrand Russell, one of five honorary chairman of the CCF, articulate what could be called the New World Order's mission statement:

> I think the subject which will be of most importance politically is mass psychology... Its importance has been enormously increased by the growth of modern methods of propaganda. *Of these the most influential is what is called "education."* Religion plays a part, though a diminishing one, *the press, the cinema, and the radio play an increasing part...* It may be hoped that in time anybody will be able to persuade anybody of anything if he can catch the patient young and is provided by the State with money and equipment.
>
> The subject will make great strides when it is taken up by scientists under a scientific dictatorship... the social psychologists of the future will have a number of classes of school children on whom they will try different methods of producing an unshakable conviction that snow is black. Various results will be arrived at. First, that the influence of the home is obstructive. Second,

that not much can be done unless indoctrination begins before the age of ten. *Third, that verses set to music and repeatedly intoned are very effective. Fourth, that the opinion that snow is white must be held to show a morbid taste for eccentricity.*

Although this science will be diligently studied, it will be rigidly confined to the governing class. *The populace will not be allowed to know how its convictions were generated. When the technique has been perfected, every government... will be able to control its subjects securely without armies or policemen.*[27]

In the same tract, Russell vociferously attacked the existence of nation states, citing them as a critical obstacle to the freedom of individuals and the possibility of world government.

The historic center of the mass psywar apparatus Russell referenced, was London's Tavistock Institute. It pioneered theories of group experience which could be used to alter the values of individuals and change the assumptions which govern society. From studies of soldiers in World War I, Tavistock theorized that by the use of terror and shock, humans could be reduced to childlike and submissive states. By controlling levels of anxiety, similar states could be induced in large masses of people. Mass media were central to creating the controlled environments essential to this process.[28]

The leading "philosophers" of the American CCF, John Dewey and Sidney Hook, brought the "Frankfurt School" social psychologists to the United States. Hannah Arendt (who had been the Nazi Martin Heidegger's lover), Max Horkheimer, Theodore Adorno,

27. Russell, *The Impact of Science on Society,* London, Allen & Unwin, 1952.

28. The LaRouche movement published groundbreaking work on the Tavistock networks in 1973-74. (See *Campaigner* magazine, Winter 1973, Spring 1974 issues.) See also the May 24, 1996 issue of *EIR,* "The Sun Never Sets on the British Empire."

Herbert Marcuse, and other members of this school deliberately concealed the fact that fascism was the product of an Anglo-American "color revolution" operating pursuant to British imperial imperatives.

Fascism was, they lied, an organic social product of reason itself, which led to authoritarianism which must be beaten out of subject populations. The same theory was applied by the British psychological warfare "de-Nazification" project on which many of the Frankfurt School, Tavistock, and Congress of Cultural Freedom experts worked. The German population, rather than the actual bankers and oligarchs responsible for World War II, was held responsible for Hitler's crimes. Roosevelt was attacked by the Frankfurt School as the ultimate American proto-fascist authoritarian. Similarly, they argued, German and Italian classical culture, the rich history of classical music and poetry essential to human creativity and intellectual progress, was a key part of the fascist development, and must be suppressed and superseded by a deliberate and "free" irrationalism, all grounded in an "erotically" and sexually obsessed culture.

Theodore Adorno, the musical theorist for this evil *Kulturkampf*, extolled atonal modern music as a critical tool in destroying rational thought. He wrote:

> *The seismographic registration of traumatic shock becomes, at the same time, the technical structure law of music. It forbids continuity and development. Musical language is polarized according to its extreme, toward gestures of shock resembling bodily convulsions on the one hand, and on the other towards a crystalline standstill of a human being whom anxiety causes to freeze in her tracks. Modern music seeks absolute oblivion as its goal. It is the surviving message of despair from the shipwrecked.*

To bring about the required condition of society, Adorno argued that all forms of beauty had to be purged. Instead he argued for a steady culture of "Top Forty" pop music and other degenerate forms of mass culture, together with deliberate promotion of the random and irrational, as the appropriate tools to attack reason and create desired levels of popular conformity.

As head of the music section of the CCF and the Frankfurt School's Radio Research Project, Adorno wrote that listeners to radio music programs, "fluctuate between comprehensive forgetting and sudden dives into recognition. They listen atomistically and dissociate what the hear. . . They are not child-like, but they are childish: their primitivism is not that of the undeveloped, but that of the forcibly retarded." The findings of the Radio Research Project, published in 1949, promoted soap operas as the ideal escapist entertainment, based on primitive repetitious themes inducing mental regression and magical thinking.

The very British Aldous Huxley, Christopher Isherwood, and Alex Korda, joined Adorno for experiments in mass entertainment in Hollywood, coordinating with the degenerate British CCF operatives W.H. Auden and Stephen Spender for this purpose. Huxley, a key creator of the rock, drugs, sex counterculture which swept the United States in the 1960s, experimented with psychotropic drugs and mass brainwashing techniques. Isherwood, in turn, explored ways to pacify society through art, citing the creation of "concentration camps without tears," as his goal.

Hollywood otherwise functioned under direct CCF censorship. For example, when Hollywood produced the film version of George Orwell's *1984*, the ending was changed in order to emphasize that the Soviet Union was guilty of the crimes envisioned there by Orwell, not the British or the United States. Similarly, the CCF itself bought the rights, wrote, and produced the screenplay for the movie version of Orwell's *Animal Farm*. Cecil B. DeMille, Daryl Zanuck, and other Hollywood notables openly collaborated with C.D. Jackson, the CCF, and the CIA.

The CCF also promoted and funded Modern Art, which, to most, exhibits nothing but rampant irrationalism and overt mental breakdown. When the CIA funding of the CCF was exposed, the CIA's Tom Braden actually argued, in the *Saturday Evening Post*, that the deliberate exploitation of irrationalism was a vivid, positive, and powerful demonstration to the captive citizens of the East Bloc. It demonstrated America's radical embrace of "freedom."

The CCF itself was the brainchild of two overlapping Wall Street/media social networks and was at all times a "joint" British-American project. The "Park Avenue Cowboys" included Allen Dulles, Frank Wisner, C.D. Jackson, Kermit Roosevelt, Tracy Barnes, Richard Helms, and Royall Tyler—all closely associated with Henry Luce's Time-Life media empire and the Rockefeller, Morgan, Harriman, and other British Wall Street financial assets. Jackson was posted as special advisor to President Eisenhower for Psychological

CC/Jeremy J. Shapiro
Theodor Adorno

John Dewey

Allen Dulles

Warfare. Here he approved the core of the CCF projects and promoted the American CCF, serving on the Board.

The second circle was posted in Georgetown and consisted of the "Sovietologists": Chip Bohlen, George Kennan, and the British "philosopher" Isaiah Berlin. Kennan was the author of the infamous "Mr. X" article in *Foreign Affairs* announcing the Cold War—his philosophy was to outdo the Russians in lies and deceit. He authored numerous National Security directives in the Truman Administration, including PSBD-33/2, establishing the Psychological Strategy Board (PSB). The first Chairman of the PSB was the advertising mogul Gordon Gray.

The PSB was charged with coordinating the psychological warfare operations of the CIA, Department of Defense, and State Department. Charles Burton Marshall, a PSB officer and whistle-blower described the PSB as being run by a group of self-appointed elites "in a manner reminiscent of Pareto, Sorel, Mussolini and so on… Individuals are relegated to tertiary importance… The elite is defined as that numerically limited group capable and interested in manipulating doctrinal matters." A PSB document from June of 1953, defined these programs as necessary to "break down worldwide doctrinaire thought patterns which have provided an intellectual basis for Communism *and other doctrines hostile to American and Free World objectives*." (Emphasis supplied.)

The CCF itself was run by Frank Wisner, originally out of the State Department and then out of Allen Dulles' CIA. The CIA's Michael Josselson worked in the CCF's Paris headquarters, heading its executive secretariat. James Burnham, the former Trotskyite, was hired as a consultant and liaison to the intellectual community. The bagman was Irving Brown, who ran CIA programs through European trade union covers and otherwise functioned in Jay Lovestone's AFL-CIO International Department. Federal Bureau of Narcotics documents link Brown to numerous mafia and drug lords in Europe, and the use of drug trafficking to fund CIA operations. Malcolm Muggeridge, a member of the CCF steering committee, was the liaison to British MI6. Muggeridge's funding conduits were Sir Alexander Korda and Lord Victor Rothschild. George Orwell's publisher, Fredric Warburg, also played an active role.

Attending the CCF's founding in Berlin in 1950 were Franz Borkenau, Karl Jaspers, John Dewey, Ignazio Silone, James Burnham, Hugh Trevor-Roper, Arthur Schlesinger, Bertrand Russell, Ernst Reuter, Raymond Aron, A.J. Ayer, Benedetto Croce, Arthur Koestler, Richard J. Lowenthal, Tennessee Williams, Irving Kristol, and Sidney Hook—"thought leaders" in social science, philosophy, history, and the arts who would shape the post-war cultural paradigm.

In early 1951, Frank Wisner traveled to London to meet with his British counterparts. Over a series of meetings, it was decided to create a flagship intellectual journal for CCF, *Encounter*, co-edited by Irving Kristol and Stephen Spender. At the outset it ran articles by Julian Huxley, Allen Tate, Lionel Trilling, Robert Penn Warren, W.H. Auden, Thornton Wilder, Jayaprakash

Narayan, André Malraux, and Guido Piovene. As time went on, CCF would add the *Kenyon Review*, *Sewanee Review*, *Poetry*, the *Journal of the History of Ideas*, *Partisan Review*, *Paris Review*, and *Daedalus* to its arsenal of journals—all of them set up to be arbiters and gatekeepers of what was and was not acceptable as artistic or intellectual endeavors.

Those who refused CCF's grants and *Kulturkampf* edicts were artistically exiled and ostracized. American CCF Board member Sol Levitas, who was editor of the CCF magazine, the *New Leader*, was tasked by Allen Dulles specifically to promote a "commission of internal security" to investigative subversive influences in the United States. This Dulles edict led, ultimately, to the J. Edgar Hoover/Joseph McCarthy "Red Scare" directed specifically at holdover allies of Franklin Roosevelt and, more generally, the American population.

The Neo-Feudal Economic Model

In 1947, a different but equally subversive Anglo-American *Kulturkampf* weapon was born—the Mont Pelerin Society. The explicit purpose of this society was to revive and spread the so-called "Conservative Revolution" as spelled out in Friedrich von Hayek's *Road to Serfdom*. Evolving directly out of the Pan-European movement, the society demanded strict monetarism, personal libertarianism, deregulation, and the replacement of the nation state with a neo-feudalist world confederation controlled by the financial elite.

Von Hayek lied that the nation state itself was the cause of totalitarian phenomena like Hitler and Stalin. He claimed that "any mercantilist nation state," such as Roosevelt's United States, invariably devolved to totalitarianism, crushing individual freedom and "free markets." Echoing Jacob Burkhardt, Friedrich Nietzsche, and Martin Heidegger, von Hayek railed against the great achievements of the Golden Renaissance and Council of Florence—the creation of the modern nation state governed by principles of natural law and the development of modern science. He rejected the idea that human individuals were capable of creative scientific discovery, and ridiculed the idea that man was created in the image of God. He attacked the American System of political economy, scrawling diatribes against Friedrich List and Henry Carey by name. Von Hayek said his intellectual father was Bernard Mandeville, an avowed Satanist, who, von Hayek claimed, truthfully, was the true intellectual forbear of Adam Smith, David Hume, Carl Savigny, Jeremy Ben-

Friedrich von Hayek

tham, and Charles Darwin.

His libertarian appeal was exquisitely profiled for the United States and its post-war cultural myth of "rugged individualism," endlessly celebrated by Hollywood and Madison Avenue propagandists in such genres as the American Western.

Contrary to libertarian myths, von Hayek was also an advocate of a strong state, especially a state which was able to resist the demands of society. He wanted a new constitutional arrangement in which only "universal laws" benefitting the globalist elites could be enacted, not laws serving "special interests" expressed by the masses. He argued that this would maximize individual liberty. The legislature passing these laws would be composed of an upper house with a small membership, an assembly of mature individuals who would be elected to long terms, such as fifteen years.

Many of the "intellectuals" around the CCF and the Mont Pelerin Society were interchangeable, such as Walter Lippmann, James Burnham, Max Eastman, and Raymond Aron. Aron, who would become a key mentor of Henry Kissinger, had carried on an intense and impassioned post-war correspondence with Nazi crown jurist Carl Schmitt, whom he exonerated. Journalists associated with the CIA's CCF and Henry Luce, held dual memberships in the Mont Pelerin Society. Sir John Clapham, head of the British Royal Society, was a member. So was Nicholas Murray Butler, the President of Columbia University and patron of the Frankfurt School. So was George Shultz, whose doctoral thesis was an unhinged attack on Franklin Roosevelt's Tennessee Valley Authority.

The Rockefeller Foundation provided grants in various forms which stimulated these activities. For example, von Hayek's sojourn at the London School of Economics which resulted in the *Road to Serfdom,* and the seminars with the other Mont Pelerin founders Frank Knight, Karl Popper, and Ludwig von Mises, were funded by the Foundation. Popper became, in turn, the philosophical mentor for George Soros, as discussed more fully below. Significant funding for this effort, particularly for the society's flagship Institute for Economic Affairs (IEA) in London, also came from a close associate of Queen Elizabeth herself. Harley Drayton, the main funder for the IEA, handled the Queen's finances at the time.

In 1956, with Stalin dead, amidst challenges from Third World countries seeking economic development, and with the emergence of a new generation on the horizon, CCF sociologist Daniel Bell took leave from his post as labor editor of Henry Luce's *Fortune* magazine to become the director of CCF's Seminar Planning Committee. In April 1957, the first seminar was held in Tokyo, entitled "Problems of Economic Growth." According to Frances Stonor Saunders, "The Conference was the precursor of the impending shift by development economists from an emphasis on *growth of per capita income* to one of the *quality of social justice and freedom as the true measure of development.*" Bell would later author *The Coming of Post-Industrial Society,* formally ushering in the so-called consumer and information society.

The Post-Industrial Society

The New Left and the counterculture which emerged in the 1960s were the synthetic ideological products of this shift. For example, the Frankfurt School's Herbert Marcuse, took leave from his job running the Central European Division of the United States State Department, and, on grants from the Rockefeller Foundation, published the critiques of "mass industrial society" which became founding documents of both the New Left and the Counterculture. Not surprisingly, "participatory democracy," which the New Left originally promoted as its founding principle, was a shop-worn idea promoted by Bertrand Russell, G.D.H. Cole, and George Orwell from Britain and by the CCF's Dwight McDonald in the United States. The goal of "personal liberation" championed by Marcuse and such associates as Norman O. Brown, set the stage for the obsessive "self-improvement" and narcissistic preoccupa-

tions of the boomer and subsequent generations.[29]

The SDS itself evolved from the Student League for Industrial Democracy—the student organization for the League for Industrial Democracy (LID)—an integral entity in the CIA's infiltration of the American Labor Movement. The Director of the LID, when the future SDS left that organization, was Aryeh Neier. Neier today functions as George Soros' right hand man in the globalist Open Society movement.

Not surprisingly, workers who still identified with economic progress, the nation state, and the legacy of Franklin Roosevelt, became primary targets of New Left students. Those workers were castigated for their psychologically "repressed" and "backward" identities. Teachers, white and black, inclined to emphasize universal values, became the targets of black activists demanding "community control" of schools.

As Lyndon LaRouche emphasized in founding documents of his organization, these "new left" ideas were drawn from the syndicalism of Mussolini's fascist state and the national bolshevism of Georg Strasser—ideas identical with what FDR's intelligence services labeled "Synarchism/Nazi-Communist." Their "community control" social structures were derived directly from Kurt Lewin's studies of the dynamics of small groups. Their smallness precludes attempts to exert major influence on actual existential issues. Setting numerous such groups into competitive contiguity, where gains by one group are at the expense of another, creates the basis for a self-policing fascist order. Atomize the subject population, set race against race, language-group against language-group, women against men, etc.—and then mobilize these groups together against mass political and trade union organizations, all under the banner of anti-authoritarianism and local community control, and you have fascism with a democratic face.

Invariably, some of these groups, impotent to generate real social progress, can and will descend to anarchism and the types of purgative violence championed by another Mussolini mentor cited by LaRouche, Georges Sorel. This phenomenon was played out fully

---

29. This movement has as its corollary the complete destruction of education. After all, why is it necessary in a devolved communitarian society? Universities are now completely infested by this cultural disease—self-esteem is the central preoccupation; the intellect in the form of challenging axiomatic assumptions, is the enemy. Trigger words, safe zones, etc., destroy any possibility of debating profound ideas about the nature of man and society. See Lukianoff and Haidt, "The Coddling of the American Mind," *The Atlantic,* September 2015.

in the 1960s by the former faction of SDS known as the Weatherman and by countless terrorist gangs which followed their model.

Similarly, the "environmentalism" so central to the counterculture, was a critical idea in Adolph Hitler's Malthusian arsenal—oneness with an overpowering and arbitrary nature which man's reason has repeatedly and criminally violated, in an illegitimate search for non-existent scientific truth. Prince Philip, who has wished to come back to Earth as a virus capable of wiping out much of humanity in order to control population, has been demonstrated to be the intellectual godfather of this movement.[30]

Thus the post-industrial consumer and service economy society emerged from a generation which had been "shocked" repeatedly as Tavistock and Theodor Adorno prescribed. President Kennedy, Martin Luther King, Robert Kennedy—all potential advocates for advancing Roosevelt's vision, had been mowed down by assassins' bullets. The nation was mired for years in the genocide of the war in Viet Nam, creating a cultural pessimism which persists to this day. Widespread use of drugs, sexual hedonism, and blaring atonal rock music produced mental oblivion in large swaths of the American population, the alienation which Adorno had pronounced as his goal.

The revelation that the entirety of post-war American culture was one intelligence community-manufactured mess, should have sparked a popular revolt, to return America to its republican roots in the Constitution's model of an educated and engaged citizenry, through its representative institutions, deliberating national and international issues. Instead, as a result of the counterculture, featuring the likes of Herbert Marcuse and others, the revelation became the cynical rationale for the edict: "tune in, turn on, drop out."

III. Fast Forward to 1981-83: Another Version of Democracy

Reactions to the shattering emergence of the post-industrial paradigm, the Watergate scandals, and the Viet Nam War, largely set the cultural terms for Ronald Reagan's ascension to the Presidency. Reagan's election was preceded, however, by a new retooling of

World Economic Forum

Samuel Huntington, Chairman, Harvard Academy for International and Area Studies, speaking during the "When Cultures Conflict" session of the World Economic Forum, in Davos, Switzerland, Jan. 25, 2004.

American "democracy" and foreign policy by the Wall Street and City of London elites.

In May 1975, the Rockefeller-dominated Trilateral Commission issued a report entitled, "The Crisis of Democracy," at a conference at Kyoto, Japan. The report, authored by Samuel Huntington, Michel Crozier, and Joji Watanuki, under Zbigniew Brzezinski's direction, recognized that the Anglo-Americans faced a governance problem in the transition to a post-industrial society.

The collapse of the Bretton Woods system in 1971, presaged by the 1965-67 recessions, resulted in a decade in which Wall Street's elite were only barely able to hold off total economic collapse, through their use of the oil shocks of the 70s and the savage wage and price austerity measures undertaken by the Nixon Administration. At the same time, Third World nations were calling for real development of their economies, in a new just economic order which would turn their economies from colonial raw-materials satrapies into modern nation states. Lyndon and Helga LaRouche played an extremely significant role in leading this fight, setting forth an agenda of great projects, debt moratoria, and an International Development Bank.[31]

Huntington warned about a "democratic surge" afflicting the United States and others. Too many people wanting too many things from government, and ultimately too much participation in government, was

---

30. See, e.g., *EIR* Special Report, *The Coming Fall of the House of Windsor*, November 1994.

31. See Matthew Ogden, "A Forty-Year Fight for a New Economic Order," *EIR*, October 24, 2014.

making governance too difficult. Expectations had to be thwarted, new counterinsurgency institutions needed to be forged. The crisis demanded corporativist solutions—what one Trilateral apologist openly called "fascism with a democratic face." One of the key proposals was a new institute for the "cooperative promotion of democracy." This proposal would come to fruition in the form of the *National Endowment for Democracy* under President Reagan.

In lockstep with these developments, the Council on Foreign Relations engaged in a set of studies modernizing the forms of the Anglo-American Empire, the "Project 1980s" prospectus of the CFR. The studies were also overseen by Brzezinski and future cabinet members of the Carter Administration including Cyrus Vance, Leslie Gelb, Richard Cooper, Marshall Shulman, and W. Michael Blumenthal. The focus of this project was countering the "Hamiltonian" pro-development perspective and demands of the developing world. The CFR proposed "controlled disintegration" of the world's industrial economies, ruralization and destruction of cities in the developing sector, and a strategic approach to Russia which would force it to limit the growth of science and technology or face general thermonuclear war. It proposed to develop and police a series of alternate paths, or "critical choices," for arriving at the specified objectives. The mandate of Anglo-American foreign policy was to compel other nations to choose among these selected alternate paths. The fact that they got to choose their own path to self-destruction constituted "democracy."

The most succinct presentation of the CFR's concerns was presented by Fred Hirsch, editor of London's *Economist* in his book, *Alternatives to Monetary Disorder*. He asserts that the central conflict in economic theory is between the American System (Alexander Hamilton, Friedrich List, et al.) and the British liberal system of Adam Smith, Ricardo, et al., and he ascribes the developing world's demand for a new economic order to the taint of the "mercantilist" American system. He claims that Russia and China also suffer from this American taint in their development proposals. He attacks Hamilton and List by name.

EIR rightly labeled the incompetence inherent in "controlled disintegration" of the world's economy as "A Conspiracy of Morons" at the time.[32] However, these morons were also murderers, bent on the genocidal goal of reducing the world's population through famines, wars, or whatever means. That policy had already been formalized the previous year by Henry Kissinger in National Security Study Memorandum 200.

In the meantime, the Trilateral Commission-sponsored Presidency of Jimmy Carter featured Wall Street's Paul Volcker continuing the relentless war on U.S. living standards through the interest rate policies he set at the Federal Reserve Bank. Working Democrats and farmers, decimated by this economic warfare and faced with a Democratic Platform which embraced the cultural priorities of the New Left, began leaving the Democratic Party in droves. The Blimps went to work building a new homogenous political culture featuring an anti-Soviet Democratic Party covering the left and center, and a Republican anti-Soviet conservative and neoconservative right. Each would endorse the free market, post-industrial society nostrums of Wall Street, and counterinsurgency operations against neutral, nationalist, or pro-Soviet regimes.

While the CCF's funding had been taken over by the Ford Foundation after its exposure as a CIA operation, it had, nevertheless, been severely weakened by its exposure as a CIA/MI6 front. Its last, grand hurrah was a conference in Princeton, New Jersey in 1968, attended by Brzezinski, John J. McCloy, and Henry Kissinger, in which its traditional liberals engaged in a brawl with members favorable to the "New Left"[33] By 1981, the "Committee for the Free World" was being founded by Midge Decter, Norman Podhoretz's wife. True to form, its founding took place in Britain, and it was thoroughly integrated with the economic shock therapy and belligerent foreign policy pogroms of Margaret Thatcher. In her founding speech, given at Leeds Castle in England, Decter raved that the West was besieged by sloth and appeasement, and that the only way to ensure the demise of the Soviet Union was war. Irving Kristol added, "Our Marines are not just for parades."

The Committee for the Free World included all of the leading political devotees of the fascist Leo Strauss in the United States, Britain, and France. It was headed initially by Raymond Aron, the Carl Schmitt groupie and disciple of Alexandre Kojève. Its funders included foundations which have long been associated with CIA projects including the Smith-Richardson Foundation, the John M. Olin Foundation, and the Scaife Founda-

32. *EIR*, "A Conspiracy of Morons," May 15, 1979.

33. See Peter Coleman, *The Liberal Conspiracy*, The Free Press, New York, 1989, pp. 239-242.

tions. The infamous Project for a New American Century organization (rightly called the "Committee to Blow Up the World") emerged from this entity for the campaign which launched the Iraq War.

In Europe, the CCF remained active under the rubric of the European Foundation for Intellectual Freedom, functioning also under the auspices of the Ford Foundation. It had based its "anti-Soviet" cultural subversion operations on the new regime of individual human rights embodied in the Helsinki accords, and the communitarian ideas of democracy emerging from the New Left. As will be seen, the entire network of dissident intellectuals associated with this movement was sold, by the Ford Foundation, to George Soros for his Open Society Foundation operations.

EIRNS/Stuart Lewis

Lyndon LaRouche and Ronald Reagan appearing at a 1980 presidential candidates debate at Concord, N.H.

As part of this retooling, George H.W. Bush, the Anglophilic traitor, and William Casey, meticulously rebuilt the Secret Government to manage the new democratic police-state before and during the Reagan Administration. While President Ronald Reagan's collaboration with Lyndon LaRouche on the Strategic Defense Initiative could have changed the course of human history for the better, and did result in the demise of the British-infested Soviet state, the Reagan Administration was, ultimately, fatally turned by an assassin's bullet and the infections of Blimp ideological diseases.

There were three initial features to this rebuild:

- *Executive Order 12333*, reorganizing, expanding, and privatizing the U.S. intelligence community;
- *NSDD 77*, rebuilding U.S. and international media and propaganda operations which had been discredited by the 1974-75 exposés; and
- The *National Endowment for Democracy*, an agency now tasked to engage in revamped worldwide regime change operations under the cover of building "democracy."

E.O. 12333 consolidated all U.S. intelligence operations in the National Security Council; authorized the NSA to engage again in warrantless surveillance so long as the targets could be described as foreign; authorized the FBI to once again engage in COINTELPRO so long as the operations were approved by the Attorney General; and, most significantly, allowed the intel-

ligence community to outsource its operations to allied agencies (such as the British) and private entities without disclosure. These private entities were called "quangos." In the name of protecting sources and methods, it was widely acknowledged that officials operating under E.O. 12333 were allowed to lie about even the existence of these operations. Many of the counterintelligence programs initiated at that time remain classified to this day, including the protocols regarding warrantless NSA surveillance. Needless to say, the Constitutional violations extant in this order only became worse after the Bush/Cheney coup in the wake of 9/11.[34]

E.O. 12233 was authored by Kenneth deGraffenreid and signed by President Reagan in 1981. Its outlines, however, had already been set in a series of seminars throughout the 1970s, run by Roy Godson at the National Strategy Information Center (NSIC), where deGraffenreid also worked. NSIC was an intelligence community asset incorporated by William Casey and funded by the Richard Mellon Scaife foundations. It is alleged to have provided the funds for Brian Crozier to reconfigure his CIA/MI6 media front, *Forum News Features*, into the Institute for the Study of Conflict, an institute deemed critical, by many, to Margaret Thatcher's election. Roy Godson's father, Joseph Godson, had played a key role in post-war CIA operations, working directly under Jay Lovestone and J.J. Angleton, serving

---

34. See, e.g., the *Washington Post* series, "Top Secret America," projects.washingtonpost.com/top-secret-america/ The *Post* series documents an astounding and huge secret spy community built in and around Washington, D.C. after 9/11.

as the labor attaché in London, and running the Labor and Trade Union Press Service which was 100% subsidized by NATO.

In June 1982, President Reagan traveled to Britain, and in speech before the British Parliament at Westminster, labeled the Soviet Union the "axis of evil" and called for a mobilization of "democracy programs" to counter it. Reagan's speech was written by deGraffenreid and Kissinger crony Lawrence Eagleburger, among others. As usual, The National Endowment for Democracy which Reagan called for, was to have a British sister institution, the Westminster Foundation, dedicated to the same programs.[35]

National Security Council Decision Directive 77 (NSDD 77), "Management of Public Diplomacy Relative to National Security (SECRET)," coordinated all-agency propaganda campaigns on behalf of U.S. national security interests. Its author was Walter Raymond, a long-time CIA propaganda specialist tasked to the White House by Donald Gregg, George H.W. Bush's assistant, and William Casey. With Raymond and cohorts running the show, such democracy stalwarts as David Rockefeller, Archer Daniel Midlands Chairman Dwayne Andreas, British wheeler-dealer James Goldsmith, and Rupert Murdoch were brought to the White House to discuss funding various intelligence projects overseen by Raymond and Leo Cherne. Cherne, the longtime ally of Jay Lovestone and founder of Freedom House, was operating at the time as Chairman of the President's Foreign Intelligence Advisory Board.

As Raymond explained his method, all news was to be painted in white or black colors—friend or foe. No nuance from reality was to interfere with this White Hats–Black Hats world. Every evil known to man was to be ascribed to the individuals wearing black hats. The standard was defined by the ability to mobilize popular rage and emotion, not anything so mundane as the truth. This was the long-time British/CIA psychological warfare/regime change method. Raymond's linguistic bible was complemented by the dumbing down of the news media, implemented in the 1970s and 80s by such figures as Roone Arledge at ABC. This linguistic dumbing-down process can be traced back to Winston Churchill's demand that the English language be reduced to 850 basic words for propaganda purposes, a project he called BASIC.

The rebuilding of the Secret Government quickly became engulfed, however, in the Bush-directed, Ollie North-executed Iran-Contra debacle, coming very close to toppling the Reagan presidency. Congressional investigation revealed not only an Administration operating, against Congressional mandates, for an armed revolution in Nicaragua, but financing its Contra army by providing missiles to Iran and, more significantly, by massive drug dealing which fueled the murderous crack cocaine epidemic in the United States. But the media's blacklisting and hyena-like attacks on reporter Gary Webb, who exposed the Contras' crack dealing and its impact, proved that "public diplomacy" was now in complete control, once again, of the U.S. news media.

The other reference point for seeing this fascist rebuild in action is the prosecution of Lyndon LaRouche, which bears some similarities, particularly in its vile and completely controlled, orchestrated, and hate-filled media attacks, to the insurrection presently confronting President Trump.[36] Richard Morris, the former aide to Reagan National Security Advisor Bill Clark, testified in court during the LaRouche cases that deGraffenreid, Godson, and Raymond were the main players in a successful campaign to destroy LaRouche's influence in the Reagan Administration. All of the social democracy/CIA apparatus played a role. Lovestone and Angleton spent their retirement years plotting against LaRouche. John Train, who managed the CCF's *Paris Review*, functioned as an early front for CIA operations, directed through George H.W. Bush's Zapata Oil, including running black propaganda ops on behalf of the Anglo-American mujahideen in Afghanistan. It was Train who orchestrated the media campaign against LaRouche. The entire prosecutorial campaign was instituted when the British demanded that the FBI go after LaRouche as someone whose activities were in line with "Soviet propaganda interests."[37]

---

35. Reagan's speech had been preceded by Henry Kissinger's infamous speech at Chatham House, admitting to the British Institute for International Affairs that during his tenure in the White House and the State Department he had functioned as a British agent, keeping the British better informed than his American counterparts.

36. See Barbara Boyd and Bruce Director, "Shut Down the DOJ's Secret Murder Machine," *EIR*, Sept. 17, 1999.

37. See Russ Baker, *Family of Secrets*, pp. 13-14; Tom Mangold, *Cold Warrior, James J. Angleton*; Ted Morgan, *A Covert Life*; and Joel Whitney, *Finks*. The Lovestone/Angleton circle also included influential cold warrior Fritz Kraemer and Senator Henry Jackson, whose Senate offices and projects trained the leaders of the neoconservative movement. The Afghan effort against the Russians, involving jihadists as America's allies, gave birth of course, to Osama bin Laden.

Case Study: The National Endowment for Democracy

The NED formally came into being in 1983 after Congress passed enabling legislation. Its structure is telling. With the conjoined operation of E.O. 12333, NSDD 77, and the NED, the possibility of media or Congressional discovery of illicit intelligence activities is effectively stymied. Relationships to operations can be maintained at multiple layers of private and public entities, creating deniability and making responsibility hard to trace or find.

2012 Munich Security Conference
Henry Kissinger

Wikipedia
Madeleine Albright

The media themselves are engaged in cross-government public diplomacy initiatives, featuring salacious, carefully composed, "newsworthy" leaks from the highest levels of government. As Walter Lippmann demanded, their stories have been prepared for them. Take, for example, Judith Miller's lying reportage for the *New York Times* justifying the Iraq War, based on selected and orchestrated leaks from high government officials. Another example is the outing of Valerie Plame, engineered by Dick Cheney.

Most significantly, under the NED, Congress, which under our Constitution should be a check on these quango operations, is instead directly involved operationally in the NED. So is the extremely diminished trade union movement in the United States, which should be a natural enemy of this leviathan.

One of the founders of the NED, Allen Weinstein, let the cat out of the bag in a 1991 interview with the *Washington Post*, stating, "A lot of what we [the NED] do today was done by the CIA 25 years ago." Weinstein has also referred to the NED publicly as the "democracy quango." In 2003, the NED claimed that it had financed and influenced over 6,000 organizations in the world.

The NED is composed of four entities: the International Republican Institute (IRI), representing the Republican Party; the National Democratic Institute for International Affairs (NDI), representing the Democratic Party; the Center for International Private Enterprise (CIPE) run by the U.S. Chamber of Commerce; and the Free Trade Union Institute, now renamed the American Center for International Labor Solidarity, run by the AFL-CIO.

Put simply, the IRI seeks to influence, train, infiltrate, and control international parties on the right; the NDI does the same on the left with specific alliances in the Socialist International. The CIPE seeks to spread the ideology of so-called "market economies" throughout the world, while opening all markets to U.S. products. One of CIPE's offshoots, Transparency International, serves as a monitor on economic activity throughout the world, and is an essential actor in most "corruption" scandals at the center of regime change operations. In 1987, CIPE was credited with transforming what was the European Management Forum into the World Economic Forum at Davos.

The Free Trade Union Institute, now suitably washed and renamed, is simply the old international section of the AFL-CIO and the CIA labor networks of Irving Brown and James J. Angleton.

There have only been three Chairmen/Presidents of the NED since 1983: Allen Weinstein; John Richardson of the State Department and of the Dulles brothers Sullivan and Cromwell law firm; and Carl Gershman. All have been associated, in one fashion or another, with the Social Democrats U.S.A. All have worked at one time or another at the CIA-created Freedom House.

The NED's roster of directors over the years is a bipartisan mélange of powerful members of the establishment: Henry Kissinger, Brzezinski, Frank Carlucci, Charles Manatt, and Paul Wolfowitz, for example, who can hardly be considered "democrats." Neither can the current Democrats in the NDI, among them Donna Brazile and Will Marshall of the Progressive Policy Institute. Brazile and Marshall are neoconservative spawn of the Democratic Leadership Council. Marshall is a founder of that body. The present head of the IRI is the self-professed defender of the New World Order, John McCain. The present head of the NDI is Madeleine "the deaths of 500,000 Iraqi children is a legitimate price to pay for the overthrow of Saddam Hussein"Albright.

The actual amount of money poured into subversion efforts by the NED is difficult to quantify. Part of its operating expenses are authorized by Congress, and go through the U.S. Information Agency and the U.S. Agency for International Development (USAID). But, it also receives direct private financial support, not only for itself but directly to its subsidiary NGOs. It is also part of the Defense Department budget. And, when actual regime change operations are underway, its NGOs, of course, receive covert funding from the CIA and from its "Five Eyes" intelligence "partners," most specifically MI6. This does not even take into account the documented use of drug monies in such operations, as was done with the Contras.

Author Thierry Meyssan has tried to track the cumulative totals in the case of Libya, estimating that over the five-year period which included the assassination of Muammar Qaddafi, "democracy promotion" was financed to the tune of $1 billion in a country which has only four million inhabitants.

The NED's color revolutions have followed a familiar script. In Bulgaria, for example, in 1990, the Bulgarians made the "mistake" of electing a majority communist parliament. While European observers declared the elections legal, the pro-American opposition screamed about fraud, and took to the streets until a pro-American was elected President. A similar regime change operation, in the form of a challenge to the results of elections, occurred in Kyrgyzstan—"the Tulip Revolution."

creative commons

Riots at Maidan square in Kiev, Ukraine, that led to the coup (above). Victoria Nuland; Assistant Secretary of State for European and Eurasian Affairs (right) distributing cookies to the Maidan square demonstrators.

It resulted in the overthrow of the elected leader, sale of the country's assets to U.S. companies, and the setting up of a U.S. military base in Manas. In 2003, in Georgia, the U.S.-backed opposition claimed fraud in legislative elections and took to the streets in the so-called "Rose Revolution." This operation was simultaneously supported by George Soros and Britain's Lord Malloch Brown. President Eduard Shevardnadze fled the country and his successor, Mikheil Saakashvili, opened Georgia up to U.S. and other Western economic interests, breaking off relations with Russia. As the economy collapsed, Saakashvili imposed a dictatorship, while still enjoying NED support, and bombed the population of South Ossetia, killing 1,600 people, most with Russian citizenship. Moscow struck back, but Georgia had already been economically devastated by the "democracy promotion" exercise.

This scenario is the pattern in case after case of these

World Economic Forum/swiss-image.ch/Photo Michele Limina
George Soros at the 2015 World Economic Forum.

democracy promotion exercises. A change of leaders from someone with whom the Blimps have a beef, to someone favored by them, followed by continuing economic devolution.

As *EIR* and others have repeatedly pointed out, the main mechanism for these color revolutions is the propaganda operations flowing from NSDD 77 and E.O. 12333. Thierry Meyssan summarizes Walter Raymond's "black hat" methods, as accusing the scapegoat "of all the evils plaguing the country for at least one generation. The more he resists, the angrier the mob gets." All available media, and planted and false stories spun endlessly through public and social media, are directed to this purpose. "After he gives in or slips away, the normal division between his opponents and supporters reappears."

The mob does not put forth a positive program for the country in question, nor does it name its own preferred choice for a new leader. That has all been prepared in advance by the NED and other controllers of the event. Witness Victoria Nuland of the U.S. State Department dictating that "Yats" will be the new leader of Ukraine in her famous and widely circulated taped conversation. This after Barack Obama's United States, in the name of democracy, consciously used neo-Nazis to foment a violent coup d'état. Nuland and the NED's Nadia Diuk were the case officers for this process.

Another aspect of this insurgency planning is the

ironically named United States Institute of Peace (USIP), created in 1984 and operating under the provisions of E.O. 12333 and NSDD 77. USIP in turn was spun off from the Albert Einstein Institute of Gene Sharp, documented by *EIR* and others as being the "color" inventor for color revolutions and the inventor of other symbols employed to rally emotional support. Sharp stated that his mentor through all his endeavors was not Mahatma Gandhi, Martin Luther King, or others who have used peaceful resistance to effect political change. It was, instead, the CCF's Sir Isaiah Berlin.

IV. Finally, the Golem: George Soros, a Case Study

EIR and LaRouche PAC have published repeated exposés of George Soros over the years. You can find almost all of our reports at larouchepub. com by typing "Soros" into the search function. Our case study here only highlights the most essential aspects of what the Soros British project is all about.

In his preface to the June 2008 LaRouche PAC dossier, *Your Enemy, George Soros*, Lyndon LaRouche compared Soros with John Perkins, the author of *Confessions of an Economic Hitman*. Perkins had, in his book, confessed his role in inducing Third World countries to accept debt slavery on behalf of the international elite. Perkins, LaRouche said, has a conscience. George Soros, LaRouche said, does not. "He does not own Obama," LaRouche noted, "other people do." But Soros was crucial to Obama's election. LaRouche characterized Soros as "a political-economic hitman, like a mafia thug sent to kill a friend of yours, but only a hitman for the really big financial institutions, hired out to rob your friends, and you, of about everything, including your nation and your personal freedom."

Soros' adolescent role under the Nazis, working under forged identity papers in his native Hungary to confiscate the property of his fellow Jews, is now very well known. In a 1998 "Sixty Minutes" interview about this perfidy, Soros stated that he had no guilt or regrets. Had he not acted in this way, somebody else would have. He said the experience had formed his character.

In 1947 Soros moved to London, matriculating at

the London School of Economics, where he became a life-long disciple of Sir Karl Popper. Popper, one of a bevy of British ideologues tormenting the human race, founded the Mont Pelerin Society in 1947, as previously noted, with von Hayek and von Mises. Popper's imperial views are otherwise illustrated by his claim that the British Empire had liberated Third World nations too soon, the equivalent of leaving a kindergarten to itself. These nations must be "civilized," by war, if necessary.

Popper's central philosophic theses, like those of Leo Strauss, are based on a complete fabrication of Plato. Where Strauss animated his neocon cult with the claim that the key to Plato was propounding the noble lie, Popper claimed that Plato actually was an advocate of dictatorship and totalitarianism, based on a very deliberate misreading of the *Republic*. In order for mankind to enjoy an "open society," *the term Popper employed*, mankind must abandon the idea that there is any ascertainable truth. There is only an evolving "experience" in which happiness can never truly be gained by humans. He ridiculed the idea of God as well as science. He was a devout follower of the cult of Aristotle, the Greek philosopher rightly ridiculed by Edgar Allen Poe as championing a "creeping and crawling" mode of inquiry, permanently trapping mankind, like animals, in the hedonistic domain of sense perception.

From London, Soros went to New York, working as a portfolio manager at Bleichroeder and Arnold, an old European firm favored by European oligarchs and custodian of the funds of the Rothschild family. In 1969, Soros left Beichroeder and Arnold, taking several investors with him to found the Quantum Fund N.V., based in the off-shore tax haven of the Netherlands Antilles. Soros has consistently structured his companies to avoid oversight by United States authorities, although he was subject to SEC investigation in 1979 for manipulating the stock of the Computer Sciences Corporation. The Open Society Fund was founded in the wake of that investigation. From 1979 to 1981, Quantum suffered major losses in bond trading. It also lost $840 million in the 1987 market crash. So much for Soros' claimed Midas touch.

Quantum survived only because of investments in it by very old and very fascist European families, including Britain's Queen Elizabeth of the House of Windsor, considered to be Europe's wealthiest individual. Quantum's directors are Swiss, Italian, and British financiers, the most important of which are the Rothschilds.

They are members of the Club of the Isles and retainers of the British royal family. Sir James Goldsmith, a frequent business partner of Soros who died in 1997, was a cousin of the Rothschild family.

N.M. Rothschild and Sons is considered by City of London sources to be one of the most influential parts of British intelligence tied to the Thatcher free-market, Mont Pelerin Society wing of the Conservative Party. Dr. Alfred Hartmann, the managing director of the BCCI Swiss subsidiary, Banque de Commerce et de Placements SA, was a board member of N.M. Rothschild and Sons, tying the Rothschilds directly to the BCCI banking scandals which came to public notoriety during the George H.W. Bush Administration. U.S. and other investigations proved that BCCI was nothing but a laundromat for drug monies internationally, which were then funneled into covert Anglo-American intelligence operations, such as Bush's Project Democracy Contra operation against Nicaragua. Indictments and continuing criminal investigations led to the closing of BCCI.

George C. Karlweiss, of the Edmond de Rothschild's Swiss Banca Privata, is said to have provided Soros significant startup money for the Quantum Fund. Karlweiss also sponsored the career of fugitive dope money launderer Robert Vesco. The very dirty-money-linked Marc Rich, who made his money in the triangular trade of weapons, oil, and drugs; Shaul Eisenberg of Israeli arms fame; and Rafi Eytan, at one time the Mossad's contact with MI6, are, according to *EIR*'s various sources, in the Quantum Fund's environs. Edgar de Picciotto, who sat on the Board of Soros' Quantum Fund, merged his Swiss Union Bancaire Privée with Edward Safra's Republic Bank. Safra was notorious for outrageous and dangerous drug, weapons, and terrorist dealings; he was ultimately murdered.

EIR's earlier work demonstrated that Soros is the visible side of a vast and nasty secret network of private financial interests, called the Club of the Isles by its members, which is headed by the Windsors, and built upon the wreckage of the British Empire after World War II. It is, in many ways, modeled on the seventeenth-century British and Dutch East India companies.

Beginning with destroying the British pound—done for Club of the Isles strategic purposes in 1992—Soros has profited from numerous speculative activities against the wealth of nation states. These operations, often characterized as hit-and-run by the financial press, are more appropriately termed smash-and-grab. Soros has at various times attacked the currencies of Britain, Thailand, Malaysia, Indonesia, Italy, Germany, and many other countries, each time reflecting current British strategic interests, and each time leaving behind a collapsed local market and financial ruin of national investors. His operation against the pound, for example, emerged from a meeting on the Queen's yacht, the Britannia, and is considered to have been an essential step in bringing about the Maastricht treaty.

So, our past work has shown, in example after example, irrefutably, that Soros is a British operation. For purposes of this report, we will focus, however, on just what the Open Society preaches—the evil ideology now being deployed against the President of the United States. As we emphasized previously, "following the money" only gets you a peek. What you find is myriad groups that have, for the most part, undergone political action training. The question is, training for what?

Ariel Gutierrez

Malloch-Brown is the British agent, who has teamed up with confessed Nazi George Soros (left).

The Economic and Cultural Looting of the East Bloc

The Open Society's operations against the East Bloc began well before the fall of the Berlin Wall. They were facilitated when Soros was handed the entire extant network of intellectuals associated with the former Congress of Cultural Freedom—the European Foundation for Intellectual Cooperation or FEIE.[38]

This grouping was a spinoff of the International Center for Cultural Freedom, based on the specific desires of the Ford Foundation for a "third generation" intellectual foundation for its insurgency operations. The subversive philosophy championed was a focus on "individual human rights" and individual human "development" against the alleged depredations of the nation state. In response to a split within the former International Center for Cultural Freedom around the rampages of the New Left, this group primarily took the side of the New Left. It is hardly accidental that Human Rights Watch (HRW), the instrument of coups against governments which buck the elites, became the key weapon of the Open Society Institute at the same time.

As previously referenced, it is run by Aryeh Neier, a former director of the CIA's student League for Industrial Democracy, which produced the SDS.

HRW and its close ally, the British Foreign Office's Amnesty International, constitute an international hit-squad against nations which oppose free trade and globalization. For example, in its 1995 "Human Rights Watch World Report," HRW launched a violent attack on those individuals and governments who shared a vision "that equates economic self-interest with the common good" and it labels that outlook a "mercantilist threat" to its concept of human rights. Singled out, in this respect, was the statement by then U.S. Commerce Secretary Ron Brown in 1994: "Our strategy of commercial engagement, is, we believe, the most effective strategy to have a positive impact on labor rights and human rights."

Soros' first effort on behalf of culturally deconstructing the Soviet Union was a university, Central European University, based initially in Budapest but with branches in Warsaw and Prague. It was staffed, for the most part, by FEIE intellectuals and other British-influenced "bread scholars" (to use the appropriate term from Schiller), and chartered by the State of New York. The university focused on promoting appropriate ideologies for controlling populations in a de-industrialized state. The central ideology preached at the CEU was "communitarianism," the "participatory democracy" otherwise associated with Mussolini's fascism and the New Left, and recently resurrected by the

38. Nicolas Guilhot, "A Network of Influential Friendships: The Fondation Pour Une Entraide Intellectuelle Europeenne and East West Cultural Dialogue 1957-1991," *Minerva* (2006) Volume 44, Issue 4, pp. 379–409.

Occupy Wall Street movement. One of the big operations of the CEU is the promotion of the notion of "ethnicity," as a defining feature of identity. Cambridge University's Ernest Gellner is considered to be the godfather of this movement. Before his death, Gellner was promoting the idea that governments should hire "social anthropologists" as chief advisors to make sense of what was going on in the world.

At the July 12-14, 1996 First Communitarian Summit in Geneva, the communitarians' modern guru, Amitai Etzioni, said: "I am very close to George Soros; we have been friends for twenty-five years." This period was, of course, the critical time for this "shaping of new paradigms" crowd. The late 1960s saw the launching of the Club of Rome (the modernizer of Malthusian genocide models), and the allied International Institute for Applied Systems Analysis (IIASA), which LaRouche identified as the key weapon subverting Soviet science. The long range plan, as previously noted, was to break down the sovereign nation state and replace it with a culture of "self-expression," "irrational individualism," and the system analysis-vectored policies of One World federalism. The purpose of the CEU was to prepare a new elite to implement these policies. It was funded not only by Soros, but also by Ford, Rockefeller, Mellon, the German Marshall Fund, the Mott Foundation, and the Washington, D.C. based Eurasian Foundation.

The CEU is deeply tied to another Soros-funded institution, the Institute for Human Sciences in Vienna, which every year awards the "Hannah Arendt" prize. Arendt's work on behalf of the Frankfurt School and CCF was seminal in the evolution of the idea that a person's assertion that there are intelligible truths is proof that the person is an authoritarian personality. The president and rector of the CEU, as of 1997, was Alfred Stephan, a collaborator of Luigi Einaudi, who sat on the board of the NED's *Journal of Democracy*.

At the same time that Soros acquired the intellectu-

EIR

Cover of the Aug. 29, 1997 EIR, *exposing Soros' pushing drug legalization.*

als from the FEIE, he "acquired" the remnants of the CIA's Radio Free Europe and Radio Free Liberty for purposes of propaganda for his operations in the East Bloc.

In 1990 Soros, always in conjunction with his British masters, such as Lord Mark Malloch-Brown, planned his assault on the Soviet economy, the so-called Shatalin Plan. Shock therapy—applied through the precepts of von Hayek and Milton Friedman, as modernized by Harvard's Jeffrey Sachs—shut down and looted the Soviet military-industrial economy. Prices were "liberalized" (they skyrocketed), state industry was entirely privatized, severe austerity was imposed, and the social safety net was cut. Soros provided minimal stipends to scientists so that they could eat but do virtually nothing else. Thousands fled to the West. Rotten deals were made to sell off strategic raw materials and society became an open field for criminal trafficking in raw materials, weapons, and drugs. In only five years, the labor force had largely shifted from production to criminal activity, the living standard plunged, and the former Soviet region saw the fastest expansion of the drug trade and drug use in the world.

Implementing Bertrand Russell's Worldview

Our previous work on Soros documented, in depth, Soros' sponsorship of drug legalization in the United States, and through his collaboration with the NED and Wall Street, the transformation of Ibero-America into one huge drug factory. Not only does Soros money flow into his Drug Policy Foundation and the Lindesmith Center, at the center of the drug legalization movement—but also, his operations with the NED, British intelligence, and Wall Street have fostered the drug trade in numerous countries, particularly Peru and Columbia. The Soros and NED apparatus have attacked all nationalist governments which went after the drug trade as authoritarian, ultimately overthrowing them.

In Peru, for example, Soros was caught directly

ANCOL/Fernando Ruiz

Richard Grasso, president of the New York Stock Exchange, embracing Raúl Reyes, negotiator for the drug-running FARC rebels, June 26, 1999.

funding pro-drug candidate Alejandro Toledo, to the tune of $1,000,000, in his efforts to overthrow Peruvian President Alberto Fujimori. Toledo's attempted color revolution, the "March of the Four Corners," was set up at a forum organized by the NED's Madeleine Albright. Albright otherwise authorized the journey of New York Stock Exchange chairman and CEO Richard Grasso to meet with and celebrate Colombia's FARC drug and terrorist gang. Soros personally invested in the Banco de Colombia of the Cali, Colombia-based Gilenski family, cited by both U.S. and Russian intelligence agencies as a drug money laundromat used for purchasing properties in Russia and Crimea.

Soros' other major cultural funding thrust in the United States has been the "death with dignity" movement—the idea that individuals wracked by disease should simply die, rather than waste society's precious resources on life-saving interventions. This is the "useless eaters" idea embraced by the eugenics societies and by Adolph Hitler.

In 2003-2004, after the initial Bush-Cheney attempt at an outright fascist coup following 9/11 had to be modified into the slow creep of a privatized and largely outsourced police-surveillance state, Soros turned his funding emphasis to the United States. As we have documented, Soros supported the British-controlled candidacy of Barack Obama, opening vital flows of funds, and himself donating extravagantly to Obama's 2008 campaign. At the same time, Soros deployed his funding, as he had in Eastern Europe, to hundreds of NGO-

type political advocacy organizations operating in Obama's orbit and gutting the traditional Democratic Party. These trainees have become the leaders of the movement now deployed under the banner, "Resist" on behalf of the same British policies elaborated throughout this report—Bertrand Russell's policies for universal fascism.

In addition to his various political training institutes, Soros has provided millions and millions of dollars—by one estimate well over $48 million dollars by 2011—to over thirty U.S. media organizations. He started by funding the *Columbia Journalism Review*, considered the standard bearer, if you can imagine such a thing, for the U.S. media. ProPublica, the Center for Investigative Reporting, the Center for Public Integrity, and the Investigative News Network all receive major funding from Soros while other funding sources for investigative journalism have completely dried up. Soros' funding also extends deeply into the major journalistic associations, the National Federation of Community Broadcasters, the National Association of Hispanic Journalists, the Committee to Protect Journalists, and the Organization of News Ombudsmen. He funds Media Matters, led by the very dirty Obama/Clinton operative, David Brock, in current operations against President Trump. He is also funding Facebook's current third-party fact-checking team, checking for "fake news."

Conclusion: What To Do

This report should disturb you and move you to action. Everything is at stake in this great moment, and victory depends, as Schiller made clear, on our citizens becoming a great people. There is a political and economic program by which we can exact a just punishment for the Blimps, making them a historical relic—something studied as a horrible historic disease, a disease which was permanently cured by human beings becoming truly human in the year 2017. LaRouche's *Four Laws for Economic Recovery*, mastered by you, is the tool kit from which a Great Renaissance can be built. That, and joining China's great offer to develop the entire world and explore space, opens an exciting future to the minds of our youth—a great purpose for what can be a wonderful life. Please join us in making that happen.

REDUCTIONISM AS MENTAL SLAVERY

When Even Scientists Were Brainwashed

by Lyndon H. LaRouche, Jr.

April 7, 2004

The subject of this report is the nature of that historically specific quality of mass-insanity which has brought the world at large into the presently erupting, global, monetary-financial, economic, and strategic crisis. This is the worst crisis in the history of modern European culture since the 1648 Treaty of Westphalia ended those monstrous, Venice-inspired European religious wars, led by Habsburg Spain, of the 1511-1648 interval. The specific tactic employed here, for addressing the present manifestation of that political mass-insanity, is to show the nature and root of the relevant mass psychological disorientation of populations and institutions. The subject is treated here from the reference-point of the reflections of the way in which that more general problem is expressed within the bounds of the established, elementary presumptions of currently taught physical science.

I situate that report from the following point of historical reference in the domain of physical science itself.

The founding and development of what became the Fusion Energy Foundation (FEF), brought into play a broad, and expanding base of task-oriented scientific and related activities. Over a period of more than a decade, this reached the level of involving more than 100,000 scientists, engineers, and other relevant persons. The growth and persistence of the influence of this association was most remarkable, until it was shut down, in 1987, by means of what was subsequently ruled, on the official record, to have been a prosecutor's fraud upon the bankruptcy court.

That was the fraud, principally against me, which had been perpetrated by a politically motivated action of the Alexandria, Virginia U.S. Attorney, Henry Hudson. That fraud was plotted and orchestrated through the guiding intention of a U.S. Justice Department team then headed by its Criminal Division head, William Weld of Boston, Massachusetts. Weld was the same wretch who had set up the situation, in October 1986, for the assassination of me and others by a large task-force of Federally-deployed armed forces. Only intervention of higher authority had prevented that mass-murder from being carried out under Weld's direction. The purpose of these interlocked, nested frauds by factions within the U.S. government, was to eliminate me physically from my established position as among leading international figures of U.S. political life. The evidence is, that the clear intent of that effort from those corrupt quarters, was to eliminate me either by assassination, or by a railroad-style trial intended to send me to die of old age in Federal prison.

The political motives of those officials and other influentials sharing that malicious intention, is abundantly clear from any informed reading of the available record and correlated other evidence.

According to the court records from 1987 and 1988, this fraud was accomplished by aid of witting complicity by the chief judge of the notorious Federal Fourth Circuit's Alexandria, Virginia court, the crucial trial judge in the relevant case. The latter complicity included that judge's infamous Rule 11 prescription, excluding even essential forms of relevant evidence from the proceedings in which the defendants in that case were railroaded, without allowing the defendants reasonable time or related elements of opportunity to prepare a competent defense against hastily presented, ac-

"One of the most prominent elements of then current world history behind the motives for that corrupt operation, had been the Fusion Energy Foundation (FEF) . . . known for its leading role in generating continuing support for my personal initiative, later adopted by President Ronald Reagan, for initiating and crafting the economic science-driver alternative represented by a Strategic Defense Initiative (SDI)." LaRouche addressed 800 business, government, and diplomatic representatives at a Washington FEF conference in April 1983.

I probably would have been murdered soon after I departed the courtroom a free man.

One of the most prominent elements of then current world history behind the motives for that corrupt operation, had been the FEF, which had been the institution which had become known for its leading role in generating continuing support for my personal initiative, later adopted by President Ronald Reagan, for initiating and crafting the economic science-driver alternative represented by a Strategic Defense Initiative (SDI), the proposal which I and President Reagan proposed to the Soviet Union,

tually fraudulent charges.[1] One of my certified prior political enemies was the foreman of that jury, who secured that position by implicitly perjuring himself in what passed for a *voir dire* proceeding on that occasion! All of this was part of corrupt, purely politically motivated operations coordinated with the notorious Internal Security section of the Justice Department. Had what was later shown to have been a pre-contaminated jury done an honest job, instead of what occurred, I would have been exonerated; but, in that case,

and to other nations, including our European allies. The proposal was made by me, and proposed to, and ultimately adopted by the President Reagan who presented it publicly to the Soviet Union on a TV broadcast of the evening of March 23, 1983.

It had been my intention in crafting that proposal, both to offer the Soviet Union a way out the expected medium-term financial crisis which menaced both super-powers (and others), while building an escape-hatch for the U.S.A. itself from the Russell-Szilard trap of "Mutual and Assured Destruction" (MAD). Notably, it had been my known international role in fostering the preconditions for both the President's launching of SDI, and my continued work on behalf of that policy after March 1983, which, taken together with my 1984 candidacy for the Democratic Presidential nomination, had been the principal among the motivating issues behind a five-year effort, January 1984-January 1989, to eliminate me physically from the world's political scene, either by long imprisonment or death. Not by accident, the deployment of the Federal forces which would have killed me by the morning of October 7, 1986, had occurred while President Reagan was on his

---

1. The indictment itself was typical of a "conspiracy theory" run hogwild. The charges against all defendants were conspiracy to commit financial fraud. The basis for the allegations presented was the financial injury done to the relevant associations by a continuing conspiracy led by the Federal government itself. This included the trial Judge Albert V. Bryan, Jr.'s own complicity, in protecting the prosecution's fraud upon the bankruptcy court, under a Rule 11 construction. That trial was scheduled to prevent a retrial of the subject of a long mistrial in Federal Court in Boston, Massachusetts, which had concluded with an affirmation of the jurors' intent to exonerate the defendants. The Alexandria, Virginia trial was scheduled by Judge Bryan to pre-empt the Boston retrial, where the defendants would have almost certainly won. See **Railroad!** (Washington, D.C.: Commission to Investigate Human Rights Violations, 1989).

"Over more than a decade, [LaRouche's Fusion Energy Foundation] reached the level of involving more than 100,000 scientists, engineers, and other relevant persons. The growth and persistence of the influence of this association was most remarkable, until it was shut down, in 1987, by means of what was subsequently ruled, on the official record, to have been a prosecutor's fraud upon the bankruptcy court." The illegal liquidation of FEF (left) in April 1987; a view of the court's reprimand of LaRouche prosecutor Henry Hudson two and a half years later.

way to Reykjavik, Iceland, where he would once again present the SDI to the Soviet Union. In fact, a television rebroadcast of the deployment against me was made in Reykjavik at the time the President was re-introducing the SDI proposal there.

The central driver of that and some of the other most notable among FEF's numerous and varied achievements, reflected my commitment to a mission-oriented dedication to the implications of reviewing the principal accomplishments of Plato, Kepler, Leibniz, and Riemann, and adopting these as the exemplary guides to creative work by our association.[2] From my vantagepoint, I would have said then, and do still today, that the most important of the contributions to that from among the professional scientists, came from the influence of the now late Professor Robert Moon. Moon, at my first meeting with him, which occurred in the context of founding what became FEF, had presented me with a case which is for me typically memorable, still today.

---

2. Later, still during the early days of FEF, it was my wife Helga's collaboration with the leading scholarly figure, R. Haubst, of the Cusanas Gesellschaft, which led to our recognition of the role of Cusa as the virtual "Rosetta Stone" which provided the key to the connection of the Greek Classic to the Fifteenth-Century Renaissance. Today, we would place Cardinal Nicholas of Cusa securely in the position of the link between Plato and Kepler in that series, as Kepler himself argued in his time.

That case was the principled significance of the Ampère-Weber-Gauss discovery, partly assisted by Bernhard Riemann, of an electrodynamic principle which the influence of the philosophically reductionist school of Lagrange, Cauchy, Clausius, Grassmann, et al. had viciously excluded from the relevant standard university curricula. This was typical of Professor Moon's courage, as a scientist, in defending what were important, experimentally unique scientific truths, against fraudulent, politically arranged conventional mythologies in science, such as that of Clausius et al.; Professor Moon's action resonates in the annals of modern science to the present day.

Overall, the work of the non-profit FEF foundation filled an important niche in the support of science during that period. The specific quality of driving force which distinguished that institution, apart from, and significantly above the sometimes remarkable contributions by other leaders of the association, was located, chiefly, in the complementary intersection of my own and Professor Moon's leading influence. The case of my unique initiative, in defining, during the 1977-1979 interval, what President Ronald Reagan later adopted publicly as what he named SDI, in his March 23, 1983 televised address, is an outcome which serves as a leading example of the characteristics of my association with the remarkable Professor Moon. It also expressed the creative scientific spirit of the association as a whole.

Reference to that experience provides a most efficient way of presenting today's subject: of showing the extent to which today's prevalent, pro-reductionist form of globally extended European culture is, quite literally, brainwashing: a brainwashing which defines the reductionism of modern Aristotelianism and the neo-Ockhamite empiricism of Venice's Paolo Sarpi, as a leading, continuing tragic factor in the life and destiny of that current of modern European civilization generally.[3] In this report, I shall now show the nature of the conditions which promote the same kinds of problems, which occur as prominent, frictional problems among the ranks of scientists and others. These were problems which stirred even the atmosphere of the work of the association itself. I shall contrast the exemplary successes of the FEF, and the basis for those persisting internal frictions which had spilled over from the existing science community generally, and shall show how that provides an appropriate reference for the subject-matter which I address in the following pages. The case of the SDI will serve as our principal point of implied reference for this purpose.

The specific historical relevance of that subject of discussion now, is the following.

---

3. The Fifteenth-Century Renaissance, which revived a previously shattered Papacy, represented a revival of a Christian Apostolic tradition whose Platonic characteristics had been stressed so emphatically by the Apostles John and Paul. The corruption which had led into the Fourteenth-Century New Dark Age, and shattering of the Papacy, was a reflection of the gnostic *ultramontane* cult of opposition to sovereign nation states, which had dominated European civilization during the hegemony of a horrid alliance of the Venetian financier-oligarchy, the Norman chivalry, and the followers of Mathilda of Tuscany. Venice's treacherous role in orchestrating the fall of Constantinople, had enabled Venice's oligarchy to effect a resurgence, especially during the interval of religious warfare, 1511-1648. It was during that interval that a continuing effort was made by the Venice-led forces to uproot the institutions of the preceding Renaissance. The philosophical corruption employed and deployed by Venice is best typified by the attack on the work of Cardinal Nicholas of Cusa by Venice's Francesco Zorzi, a hater of modern science, and the marriage counsellor to England's Henry VIII, who led in demanding the supremacy of Aristotle against Plato and the early Apostles; and, the later "lord of Venice," Paolo Sarpi, who concocted a modern empiricism modelled upon the lunatic medieval doctrine of William of Ockham (Occam). It was the same Venice, as typified by the roles of Zorzi, Plantagenet pretender Cardinal Pole, and Venice-trained Thomas Cromwell, which orchestrated those schisms in the Christian church which were exploited to cause and promote the religious warfare of the 1511-1648 interval.

1. The Cultural Crisis of the Recent Century

The disorder, and induced boredom which pollutes much of the teaching of physical science today, is not a failure of science as such. It is the result of a more general, underlying disorder: a disorder of a type which has flowed into the work of scientific teaching, from the more widespread, recently accelerated cultural pessimism of the society in which that teaching is practiced. In attacking the most typical frauds met in the modern mathematics classroom, the same fraud against the calculus to which Carl Gauss pointed in his 1799 exposure of the hoax of Euler, Lagrange, and others, we discover that the belief which compelled an otherwise skilled mathematical formalist, such as Leonhard Euler, into his stubborn, maliciously motivated folly on this issue, is not a product of physical science, but, rather springs from certain dark, dank, and putrid waters of belief; from sources which have nothing to do with the generally assumed subject-matter of physical science itself.

It were impossible to locate and understand the axiomatically underlying sources of Euler's relevant pathological conceit, without focussing on its roots in an axiomatic irrationality. This irrationality influenced the Twentieth Century in an extreme way, through the influence of such radicals as Bertrand Russell and his clones. Typical of those clones, is the way in which Wiener and von Neumann polluted the Twentieth Century's classrooms; it is a corruption which has spilled over, as those same pathological influences, into the present young century. That pattern of corruption, as it is encountered in Euler, or the influence of radical positivists Russell, Wiener, and von Neumann today, can not be competently understood without treating the issues involved as a process of ebbs and flows, since as far back as the birth of European science as pre-Euclidean Classical Greek philosophy. I trace that connection here.

So, working within the context of globally extended European cultures since ancient Athens, the cause for the perennial failure of what is called "democracy," is the axiomatic substitution of a modern form of sophistry which often passes for widely accepted mere opinion—such as an *a priori*, fallacious type of axiomatic opinion. Typical of this in modern times, is the method of Descartes, which he and his followers have in place of the function of a scientifically validatable principle of truthfulness.

When we say "democracy," we intend to refer to the increasing participation of the entirety of a society, in deliberations on all important matters of policy. There is no doubt that the birth of the modern European nation state in the Fifteenth-Century European Renaissance, unleashed a kind of relative democratization which has been an indispensable factor in all general improvements in the productive powers of labor, standard of living, and degree of political freedom which have occurred since. Indeed, in no part of history of humanity as a whole, has society's progress in these matters matched the pace and scope of the benefits unleashed by that Renaissance.

This continuing progress in modern European civilization, until recently, must be traced in the history of government itself. This superiority in progress, over all known preceding forms of society, has been due to the establishment of the first modern nation states, Louis XI's France and Henry VII's England. The possibility of creating such nation states depended, in turn, on the premises defined by the preceding, great ecumenical Council of Florence in which Nicholas of Cusa played a crucial kind of specific role. Studying the same matter more deeply, the adoption of that Socratic principle of *agapē* which was promoted, most notably, by the Christian Apostle Paul's **I Corinthians** 13, as the notion of the *common good*, or *general welfare*, is the foundation upon which instances of the sovereign nation state's healthy existence, and persistence, have depended, without exception, still today. This is the same principle identified by Gottfried Leibniz, as that notion of the *pursuit of happiness* conveyed into the founding of U.S. Independence, from Leibniz's attack, in his **New Essays on Human Understanding**, on John Locke's decadent, pernicious views.[4]

The Platonic conception of *agapē*, as recognized as a matter of principle by Christianity, is properly identified as the fundamental constitutional principle of a true republic in general, and a modern democratic form of constitutional republic in particular. This principle is central to the U.S. Declaration of Independence and to that statement of intent governing the existence of the U.S., which is the Preamble of the Federal Constitution.

This concept, as underscored by Leibniz, rests upon *the principled nature of the absolute difference between human and beast. That is a revolutionary point of difference between us and the lower species of life, a difference which is expressed essentially by the human individual's unique capacity to discover and employ efficient universal physical principles whose existence can not be directly accessed by sense-perception.* It is through the exercise of that sovereign capacity of the individual person, that mankind has risen to levels vastly above the potential relative population-density which had been possible under the fixed potential for a species of higher ape. This activity is the soul and essence of physical science.

It is in the pursuit of the fruitful expression of that same specifically human capacity reflected as fundamental scientific progress, and also in other ways, that mortal man touches immortal happiness. The promotion of the rights of mankind so endowed, so allowed, is the principled basis for the sovereignty of the republic. It is the basis for the principle of promotion of the general welfare, and, therefore, of the means to fulfil the duty of the living to better the welfare of their posterity.

It is through those processes of communication, which are typified by the Platonic form of Socratic dialogue, as typified by valid methods of physical science, that the people of a society are enabled to generate, and to replicate valid discoveries of universal physical principle. The definition of truthfulness, both for science, and otherwise, lies exactly here.

The idea of "democracy" is a morally and functionally valid one, only if we mean a society which is dominated by that principle of dialogue represented by Plato, which is truthful; rather than a beast-like society ruled by the tyranny of so-called popular or kindred forms of mere opinion. If "democracy" signifies the pursuit of truth as Plato's Socratic principle defines this; democracy were noble. If it signifies the substitution of mere opinion for Socratic dialogue, then, as the judicial murder of Socrates attests, a democracy ruled by the tyranny of mere opinion, as at Athens then, is evil, and dangerous to the society of its believers. This is shown for the case of the ancient Athens of Pericles and Thrasymachus, by the doom of that city—which had been, prior to such corruption, the noblest and best expression of the upward impulse of Classical ancient

---

4. See Philip Valenti, "The Anti-Newtonian Roots of the American Revolution," **EIR**, Dec. 1, 1995.

Greek society—through its criminality in launching and conducting the Peloponnesian War.[5]

The controlling presence of evil in a society was typified then, by the systemic irrationality of the Delphi cult, and of philosophical reductionists such as the Eleatics and their successors, such as the Sophists and Aristotelians. In modern Europe, evil as typified by the influence of the empiricist followers of Venice's Paolo Sarpi, is typical of the early influence of such mental disorders in the roots of European culture today. The principal errors in ideas about science today, are to be traced from a general moral failure within U.S. society, increasingly, over the lapse of time, to date, since the untimely death of President Franklin Roosevelt. To understand the relevant causal connections for this kind of decadence, we must abandon the foolish habit of considering currently prevalent practices as being "normal" simply because they happen to be currently prevalent. We must recognize, and confess, that, often, the name of "democracy" is used as if it were a surrogate for the arbitrary power of an emperor, king, or tyrant. Often, the tyranny of a popularized false opinion, the tyranny of forms of widespread irrationalism, became the instrument by which the majority of a people may do a willful injury to themselves as grievous as might, otherwise, be expected of a lonely dictator.

The human species is intrinsically good, when it is true to itself. Contrary to preacher Jonathan Edwards and his followers today, God does not have bad taste. Man is, by nature, the noblest and best of all living creatures. It fails to be its good self, when it permits its passions to bring it to descend into infantile beastliness, as populism typifies the most common form of that moral corruption which has sometimes led from populist notions of democracy into fascism. On this account, as in the United States itself, the degradation of the behavior of a great people and nation is the consequence of a lack of exceptional men and women, who, in becoming leaders, are able to bring out the better qualities of their people. Often, the doom of a great nation is the result of either a lack of such leaders, or their rejection by corrupt populist littleness of the people, as in the case of the Athens of Pericles, or the slide of pre-1939 Germany or Italy into fascism and world war.

Abraham Lincoln's famous warning typifies the problem for the case of the U.S.A.: You can fool all of the people some of the time, and some of the people all of the time, but you can not fool all of the people all of the time. Lincoln's warning sums up the U.S. republic's internal experience, the ebbs and flows of our shifts from achievement, to lunacy, back to achievement, and so on, over the entire span of that people's experience, from the beginning of that republic, through the present day. In a constitutional republic such as ours, no tyrant can prevail for a significant time, unless the majority of the people themselves have been first become corrupted, as today, to an effect coinciding with Lincoln's famous aphorism.

The art of tyranny is: Corrupt the people first, and they will probably come to accept, or even demand the tyrant. The deep cultural pessimism fostered in Germany's post-war population of the 1920s, generated the potential which Britain's Montagu Norman and others exploited to place Adolf Hitler in power. The populists' deluded faith in their perverted definitions of "democracy," is the cherished delusion, that tyrants come to power by acting against the will of the people. Exactly the opposite is true; It is the corruption of the opinion and morals of the people, which paves the broad highway down which the tyrant marches to triumphant acclaim by the popular will, as Hitler did in Germany, and elsewhere. Later, the foolish people who cheered for the rise of the tyrant, may come to regret what they have done; but, even then, they will rarely allow that bitter lesson to remind them that, essentially, they did this to themselves.

Thus, as in the notable case of Nazi Germany, the tyranny of popular opinion may lead to a people's imposition of an incarnate tyrant, and perhaps, also, an incurable system of tyranny, upon themselves. The means by which a people's popular opinion brings a monstrous tyranny upon them as in that case, is the adoption of a Romantic's sort of entertainment-oriented fantasy life, such as what is expressed in the pathology

---

5. Typical of the category of absolute denials of the existence of truth, is the case of the "Frankfurt School" elements of what are fairly described as fascists such as, notably, Theodor Adorno and Hannah Arendt, and the school of drama of the frankly diabolical Bertolt Brecht. The existentialists, such as Arendt's Nazi intimate Martin Heidegger, based their so-called philosophy on an explicit denial of the existence of truth. In the case of Arendt, she based her denial of the existence of truth, on the reading of Immanuel Kant by Karl Jaspers. Her argument was a correct reading of the implications of Kant's doctrine. This denial of truth, as by her, formed the based for the pernicious, implicitly Nietzschean doctrine of The Authoritarian Personality, and related sophistry expressed as ritual, hyperventilated chants against "conspiracy theories," which has been deployed in the United States since the late 1940s. Cf. Lyndon H. LaRouche, Jr., "When Economics Becomes Science," **EIR**, Dec. 18, 1998.

of a mass of screaming fanatics at a sports event, such as feeding Christians to the lions in ancient Rome, or a Nuremberg rally in Hitler's Germany. It is the substitution of what is, or pretends to be a democratic quality of popular opinion, for truth, which is the usual root of a people's self-inflicted tyrannies. The United States, among others, has been experiencing a decades-long repetition of that kind of long wave of alternating surge of flow and temporary ebb of a continuing flood of corruption by such tainted popular opinion.

Therefore, in the history of modern Germany or the U.S.A., for example, the study of how corruption of the greater mass of popular opinion, as in the United States recently, creates the appetite for a threatened or actual tyranny, as today, must be a foremost concern of the study and application of political science. In this report, I reference a crucial aspect of the recurring experience of this problem which had to be overcome, again, and again, in each step forward made by FEF. I reference that experience here, to go, as directly as possible, to the inner core of that recent and continuing, British Fabian Society-like corruption of popular opinion, the which is the leading source-cause of the presently immediate internal threat to the continued survival of the U.S.A—and also, the United Kingdom itself.[6]

The scientists most attracted to FEF were drawn from men and women of an exceptional quality of development of their character, like physical chemist Robert Moon, as in our men and women of notable achievements in the domain of experimental physical science. It was the same in Europe in the past, and is expressed in a comparable fashion, to my personal knowledge of the situation, among the surviving leading scientists of Russia today. In the laboratory, or comparable settings, they were excellent models of the role of the Platonic method of hypothesis in the work of dis-

LaRouche's most valued collaborators in the varied scientific work of the Fusion Energy Foundation included leading veteran scientists of the nation's wartime Manhattan Project, such as the late Dr. Robert Moon, developer of a new model of the atomic nucleus.

covering universal physical and related principles. They were able, as experimentalists, to conceptualize a unique demonstration of a principle, not as a mere mathematical formula, as if at the customary mathematician's blackboard, but as a definite object of the mind, as what Riemann defined by his qualified use and application of Herbart's notion of *Geistesmasse*.[7]

---

6. The U.S. defeat, under Lincoln, of the treasonous, London-sponsored Confederacy, established us as a nation too powerful to be destroyed simply by repetition of that kind of subversion. So, the British successors of Lord Shelburne's Jeremy Bentham and his Lord Palmerston adopted a modified approach to the same ultimate end, an approach which became known as the Fabian Society of such leading notables as the utopian protégé of Thomas Huxley, H.G. Wells, and U.S.-hater Bertrand Russell. The Blair government at 10 Downing Street today, with its shamelessly intimate, Fabian Society ties to its accomplice U.S. Vice-President Dick Cheney, is a nest of such war-like, lying, virtual fascists of the Wells-Russell tradition, fascists strutting in New-Left-wing costumes today. Of the Downing Street-Cheney intimacies, it may be fairly said, that a buzzard which flies on two left wings, tends to veer to the far, far right, when careening in search of its beloved carrion.

---

7. Cf. Riemann, **Werke**, H. Weber, ed. (New York: Dover, 1953), *Anhang*. The name of an experimentally validatable universal physical principle is not a card-index guide to a mathematical formula on file. The name of the principle is the name of the actual physical object as a mental object, and the mathematical formula is merely the description of *the shadow* of the object. The idea of that object is associated with the willful setting of the object into efficient motion; the mathematics is an effort to describe the behavior of that object (i.e., a Pythagorean-Platonic *power to act*) when it is set into motion. This notion was introduced to policies of education by Herbart; Riemann found in Herbart's Göttingen lectures the psychological key to defining the anti-Euclidean physical geometry of his 1854 habilitation dissertation. Thus, as Riemann emphasized in that location, he carried forward to its necessary further development, the notion of an anti-Euclidean geometry which Carl Gauss had developed under the tutelage of the great Eighteenth-Century mathematicians Kästner and Zimmermann. Riemann's notion of *Geistesmasse* is key for understanding the adoption of Riemann's integration of the germ of the higher geometry of Abel's work into his own work. This notion of *Geistesmasse* is also key to understanding the application of my own contributions to a science of physical economy. This corresponds to the requirements of Riemann's notion of the geo-

The Trouble With Science Today

The trouble for many of these good scientists has often erupted, when the time came to submit an experimentally solid discovery of theirs to that virtual "Babylonian priesthood" to whom the accepted practice of today's society has entrusted the contemporary defense of the rabidly reductionist faith of "generally accepted classroom mathematics," the faith of Newton, Euler, Lagrange, et al. In short, with the ascent of those empiricists, "Things suddenly turned weird!" As Carl Gauss showed, in his 1799 attacks on the cardinal follies of Euler, Lagrange, et al., this was something external to physical science, something smacking of the quality of the same kind of evil which was the Spanish Inquisition of that rabidly anti-Semitic Thomas Torquemada who was adopted as a model for what was to become the fascism of Adolf Hitler, adopted by the intellectual, satanic founder of what became modern fascism, the Savoyard Martinist freemason, Joseph de Maistre. So, often, an evil influence had intruded along the march from the experimental laboratory to the Babylonian priesthood's torture-rack, the mathematical reductionist's "generally accepted classroom" blackboard.[8]

The existence of this intruding external evil, this generally traditional, but pathological division of science from art, is the object which Britain's notable C.P. Snow described as the paradox of "two cultures": physical science versus the rest.[9]

In effect, what Snow pointed toward, is the fact that the name of physical science is customarily assumed to bear the burden of representing a meaningful, experimental standard of truthfulness; whereas, popular opinion, and the currently popular opinion respecting the arts, tend toward enjoying the privilege of considering acceptable whatever a kaleidoscopically turbulent mass of evolving, currently fashionable opinion chooses. When experimental science is compelled to share the same bed with the widespread irrationalism of generally accepted, and academically taught "liberal arts" today, truth has been thrown out the window, and who knows what foul mental diseases (such as existentialism) may come in. The meaning of scientific "truthfulness" in general, is either degraded to a matter of a witness' crude, naive notion of sense-perception; or, it may appear as a theorem of physical science as explained at the blackboard in terms of "generally accepted classroom mathematics."

This is not only the exclusion of truthfulness from science; but, from opinion generally—as today's press is mostly freed from the encumbrance of laws banning maliciously reckless disregard for truth. As a consequent replacement for truth, we have such abominations as opinion by a chiefly lying press. Crooked courts, or, official decrees by lying official perverts, are typical of many cases in which the replacement of any kind of truthfulness, has occurred by the authority of mere opinion. In modern experience, when the standard of so-called scientific truthfulness itself is systemically false, it were more or less inevitable, as today, that no reliable standard of truth will long prevail in public affairs. Thus, as U.S. President Abraham Lincoln said famously: The substitution of a sophistical kind of popular opinion has been repeatedly the chief agency of moral corruption in recent generations, as, again, over the recent four decades now.

The role of that kind of corruption in the practice and teaching of science, provides the relatively simplest demonstration of the principled source of the tendency for corruption which is, otherwise, currently rampant in virtually all aspects of social life. The refusal, or simple evasion of the moral obligation to deliberate the launching of a policy of practice according to the Platonic principle of Socratic dialogue among those choosing a course of action, is the typical result. Today, that is the most frequent cause for prevalence of the inanities and outright evils which may be perpetrated by, and within a so-called "democratic" society, or a free association of any kind within society. This kind of widespread perversion, is what I shall refer to, below, as the kind of general pathology which I identify as a "fishbowl" mentality.

---

metrical principles of Abelian, multi-phase-spaced functions for conceptualizing V.I. Vernadsky's functional notion of the Noösphere, and for an appreciation of my own view of Vernadsky's explicit reliance on Riemann. There is an ongoing pedagogical series on this implication of Riemannian Abelian functions, which is being conducted as an educational program among my associates.

8. I acknowledge my borrowing this usage of "Babylonian priesthood" from J.M. Keynes' published report on his examination of the contents of that famous chest of Isaac Newton's scientific papers. Keynes reported, that this chest, whose contents had not gone through any supposed fire, contained no hint of Newton's actual tendencies to discover a differential calculus, but, rather, was a collection of some of the worst sort of black magic in the form of medieval alchemy. For example, this same term used by Keynes was also employed, independently, by others, at a notable meeting of some FEF veteran scientists at Ibykus farm at the close of 1988.

9. C.P. Snow, **Two Cultures and the Scientific Revolution** (London and New York: Cambridge University Press, 1993 reprint).

A typical, concentrated expression of this, is the application of the immoral, sophistical doctrine of legal "finality" to instances such as executions of condemned persons, even when the facts prompting the judicial decision were discovered to contradict the claims on which the previous decision had been based. Such and kindred uses of "finality"—as in the case of the sophist Justice Antonin Scalia's Pontius Pilate-like intervention in the matter of the 2000-2001 Presidential succession, or the similar practices of the evil murderer and torturer, the anti-Semitic Spanish Inquisition's Thomas Torquemada—are often shown by experience to have been the cruelest crimes against humanity, and even an entire society.[10]

Reflection on this problem prompts us to define, and then combine the implications of two questions. First, what is the physical standard of truth which should be superimposed upon "generally accepted classroom mathematics"? Second: what is the comparable, appropriate standard for matters other than physical science? Third: how are the two standards to be reflected as a single principle of truthfulness governing both? Those

are the intertwined questions which I address in terms of the lessons to be adduced from the starting-point of my own and FEF's experience with the development of what became known as the U.S. Strategic Defense Initiative (SDI).

1.1 The Continuing Utopian Menace

Now, against the background of the argument here thus far, let us turn our attention to a leading aspect of the way in which the kind of problem, the problem represented by a surrogate for religious fanaticism, the continuing menace of strategic utopianism, which we have identified, has become a dominant feature of world events today. I shall situate the continued importance of my proposal for what became known as the SDI at a later point in this report, against the background I shall summarize here, now.

The matter we are considering in this report is not only complex, but the complexities themselves are an indispensable, essential part of a subject which is little understood, but on which the successful outcome of the present crisis depends. For example, as we turn now to the political source of the present world crisis, the cultural impact of the British Empire on the world's physical science and political culture, the reader should not forget that the point toward which we are working here, is the social-political motive for that Empire's tendency to suppress all competent knowledge of both the underlying, controlling principles of effective science, and also of the nature of truth in artistic culture and political practice.

The question we must pose, and answer, as I do that in this report, is: *What were the forces in modern history which, in effect, considered it necessary for their continued political power, to uproot the idea of truth as a systemic principle?* The solution for that riddle, of how the systemically pathological features of modern culture were embedded, is found in the systemic, empiricist features of the 1763-2004 history of the continuing British Empire and its impact on the world as a whole, especially upon globally extended European culture.

With this purpose in view, look now at certain characteristic features of Twentieth-Century history as a bench-mark for study of the cultural problem of globally extended modern European civilization as a whole.

The Twentieth Century as a whole should be remembered by future historians as, chiefly, the symbol—if but a mere part of a more than a century-long single

---

10. It is emphatically relevant to the point being developed in this present report, that the report that it was "the Jews" who were responsible for the Crucifixion of Jesus Christ, is not an expression of opinion; it was a falsehood spoken out of malicious disregard for truth. Under Roman imperial law, the only authority which could order a public crucifixion was the Roman Emperor; in this case, the Tiberius reposing at Capri during the time of Christ's crucifixion. The only authorized surrogate for Tiberius present in Judea at that time, was Tiberius' son-in-law, the Procurator Pontius Pilate. Pilate's motive for his order in this case was that Jesus was a Jew, specifically one with the rumored reputation of being an insurrectionary "King of the Jews," ostensibly the pretender of a Jewish population largely in a state of virtual revolt against the Roman occupation forces. The Jewish "Quislings" who howled for Christ's death, were the collaborators of the Roman occupation. Nero later crucified the Apostle Peter, on a related charge, as the Apostle Paul was also murdered by Rome for the same continuing reason of Rome's imperial policy. The crusades, including the Albigensian crusade and the Norman conquest of Anglo-Saxon England, were an expression of the fraudulent, actually Roman, not Christian, *ultramontane* legacy of the doctrine of Pontifex Maximus, as under Roman imperial law. The Inquisition under Torquemada was an expression of the same heathen bestiality expressed in the Norman Inquisition's burning alive of Jeanne d'Arc. The fraud, that the crucifixion of Christ was a Jewish conspiracy, was concocted as a cover for what became the so-called *ultramontane* dogma which dominated the medieval period associated with that Venice-Norman-Cluniac-Welf alliance, whose fraudulent "donation of Constantine" myth was a device for attributing the origins of the Christian church not to Christ and the Apostles of his generation, but, rather to contrary purpose, rooting the authority of the church as an opponent of the existence of sovereign nation states, in the church's allegedly imperial, integrist legitimacy within the Pantheon of the Roman imperial doctrine. Such is the evil of mere opinion.

Gorbachev (left) and Reagan (under picture) met in Reykyavik, Iceland in October 1986. Not only did this summit founder over Gorbachev's rejection of the SDI—confounding 1,000 journalists who were misled as to its importance—but during that summit week, LaRouche was nearly killed during massive government raids, involving hundreds of armed agents, directed against offices and residences associated with him in Leesburg, Virginia.

source—of the persistently recurring periods of tragedy experienced by globally extended European civilization. At the start of this tragedy, there was the deep-going cultural decadence which accompanied the Edward VII-led, 1892-1904 onset of World War I, and the 1920s aftermath of that war. For our purposes in this report, it is sufficient to focus on the later portion of that process, its recent eighty-odd years of history, the period since the infamous Versailles Treaty which bridged the connection between two World Wars, and also laid the basis for the present threat of a global form of spreading asymmetric warfare, a form of warfare which might be the world's plunge into a protracted new dark age comparable to that of Europe's Fourteenth Century.

The key to most of the past seventy-two years of world history, since the March 1930 fall of Weimar Germany's Hermann Müller government, is expressed, in a concentrated way, in the crisis-reeking early years following the initial outbreak of the Great Depression. The most crucial turn is located between, on the one side: Germany's capitulation to Adolf Hitler's appointment as Chancellor, on Jan. 31, 1933, and Hermann Göring's Feb. 27, 1933 Reichstag Fire; on the opposing side: the inauguration of U.S. President Franklin Roosevelt, at a time just shortly after that assumption of dic-

tatorial power by Hitler. It was Hitler's rise to power, through the infamous *Notverordnung* issued on the pretext of the Reichstag Fire, then, at a time even prior to Roosevelt's inauguration, which made World War II, or some variant of it, inevitable. Worse: Had Hoover, rather than Roosevelt, been elected, or had Roosevelt not survived the high risk of assassination, to be inaugurated, Hitler or his imperial successors might be ruling the world today.

That conflict between the policies of Hitler and Roosevelt has persisted to the present day, today, and is more acute, more ominous than during any time since the British Prince of Wales, later King Edward VII, began organizing Europe, beginning 1892-1904 developments in France, and by aid of the Fashoda incident of 1898, for what would become the so-called World War I. The most crucially relevant connections are, very briefly, as follows.

The Role of the British Empire

To understand the issues underlying that war, and the parallel threat represented by the Dick Cheney-Tony Blair echo of Hitler today, we must focus our attention on an institution, the France-Savoy-based Martinist freemasonic order, created by the British East India Company of Lord Shelburne's time, the freemasonic order which pre-organized both the French Revolution against Louis XVI, and the dictator Napoleon Bonaparte, and which produced, later, the Synarchist organization which organized the post-Versailles, fascist takeover of western and central continental Europe, during the 1922-1945 interval. The issues which prompted the Synarchists of 1919-1945, to organize the fascist regimes of that period, are the same issues of international private banking which are behind the roles of Tony Blair's 10 Downing Street and Vice-President Dick Cheney, as also Hjalmar Schacht-like George Shultz, and kindred scoundrels today.

It must be understood, that the British East India Company was an outgrowth of the neo-Venetian Anglo-Dutch banking-commerce associations, which had established the previously-planned British monarchy with the 1716 accession of George I. This was not merely an echo of the former character of Venice as a financier-oligarchical form of maritime power; it was a creation of those financier and related interests of Venice, which chose to reincarnate a thing in their likeness in the seas and related coastal areas of Northern Europe. In a typically Venetian way, that British private Company contrived to set the rest of continental Europe into what became known as the Seven Years War, a war against Frederick the Great's Prussia by every other power of the European continent. In the process, while France was distracted by this continental enterprise, the diligent British East India Company effectively took over India and grabbed France's principal territories in North America. As a consequence, the victory of the British East India Company in the 1763 Treaty of Paris, established the Company as the de facto British Empire which continues to exist, if in a tattered form, to the present day.

This idea of empire, as sketched by Lord Shelburne's lackey Gibbon, used the Venetian faction of the founder of empiricism, Paolo Sarpi, and, later, Paris-based Abbé Antonio Conti, to create the Martinist cult of the circles of Voltaire, d'Alembert, Cagliostro, Mesmer, et al., and, most notably, the most Satanically evil Savoyard, Joseph de Maistre, in France. This British-sponsored freemasonic interest, assisted by Shelburne's personal assets Necker and Philippe Egalité, pre-organized and conducted the French Revolution launched on July 14, 1789, while Shelburne's lackey Jeremy Bentham deployed British agents such as Danton and Marat, trained in and dispatched from London, to unleash what become known as the Jacobin Terror. Bentham, who earned the British Foreign Office its international notoriety during the ill-conceived remainder of his lifetime, created Lord Palmerston, and set the stage for Palmerston's launching of Mazzini as his puppet and controller of the Young Europe and Young America operations which toppled Britain's rival, Metternich, and put British agent Napoleon III on the throne of France. This set into motion what became that Confederacy which was intended to destroy the United States and to balkanize the remains of both the U.S.A. and other nations, such as Mexico, into a condition of squabbling local tyrannies suitable for British management of the Americas as a whole.

Given the unpleasant end of Shelburne's chosen model, the Roman Empire, Shelburne was at great pains to discover means by which such a doom as overtook that earlier empire might not overcome the recently born British East India Company's empire. To this end, the pathetic Mr. Gibbon was employed as Shelburne's scholarly, if emotionally disturbed lackey. Both Gibbon and the German Mommsen, are typical of the ideologues who managed the misleading accounting of history since ancient Greece, in a way intended to make the universe perpetually safe for an eternal British Empire.

These facts must not be read as presuming the existence of some primary British interest contrary to the tradition of the Venetian financier-oligarchy. The British East India Company, and its new empire, were then, and remained, the embodiment of a far-flung, international financier-oligarchical interest according to the Venetian model imported to England, among other places, by such notable Venetian Satan-helpers as Francesco Zorzi, the marriage-counsellor of Henry VIII, and, the Paolo Sarpi who launched English empiricism through notable assistance from such of his protégés as Galileo, Francis Bacon, and Thomas Hobbes.

Those leading features of that Venetian model adopted by England and the British monarchy later, are relevant to my development of the proposal which became known as President Reagan's public proposal of the SDI to Soviet General Secretary Andropov. The crucially relevant features of that proposal, are essentially two.

First, the British imperialists' conviction, that the potentially powerfully challenging forces of the Eurasian continent and the Americas, must be repeatedly set at one another's throats in such a way as to prevent the emergence of any power in the world which might be a capable threat to the continued existence of the empire which Shelburne had led in his time. World War I is a prime example of this British strategy (the slaughter of Britons in that war was a matter of the regime's relatively cheerful indifference to the interests of the British population; it was the City's "Old Lady" and what she represented, not human interests, which were intended to be served in such a gruesome fashion. For the "Old Lady," sacrifices must, obviously be made, when the occasion appears to warrant this service to cause of perpetuating the empire.)

The present threat of a fascist coup in the U.S.A., such as one by forces associated with Dick Cheney and

George Shultz, and the echoes of Lazard Frères' pre-1945 France, goes to the heart of the second principal feature of the Shelburne policy-model.

On this second account, the kind of Anglo-Dutch Liberal model which reigns in western and central Europe today, is based on three elements which pass for "constitutional" among the credulous sorts of victims of such arrangements. One, obviously, is the non-parliamentary state apparatus. The second, is the parliamentary government, which is readily overthrown whenever the emergence of a crisis prompts the bankers to demand such adjustments. The third is the equivalent of what is commonly recognized today as an independent central banking system, which is the part of the government which is owned by the Venetian-style, international financier oligarchy, and which often prevails over state and parliament, as it did, so often, in continental Europe between 1922 and 1945.

However, for all nations, whether of the Anglo-Dutch Liberal model, or not, the kinds of international financial systems existing still today will, by their nature, lead repeatedly to the kinds of financial-monetary crises in which the bankers install a fascist dictatorship, or the equivalent, in order to ensure that the bankers, not the people, will be saved as financial powers, even if the people must be forced to die en masse to bring that happy financiers' remedy about.

Hence, since the establishment of the Venice-style of neo-Roman, British empire-in-fact, by the relevant 1763 Treaty of Paris, the world has been dominated *politically* by the ebbs and flows of either cyclical or systemic financial-monetary crises, as the world is presently dominated by the onrush of, *not a cyclical*, but a *systemic crisis* of the monetary-financial-economic system as a whole, an immediately threatened general breakdown-crisis. Among leading political and financial circles around the planet, many presently acknowledge this privately, although many of them, for reasons of political discretion, and reflections on the risks inherent in mortality, lie their heads off about this matter publicly.

These key features of Anglo-Dutch Liberal culture to date, are to be understood as the political and cultural reflection of, chiefly, the empiricist dogma introduced to Europe by Venice's Paolo Sarpi. Empiricism is a modern echo of the ruinous reign of sophistry by which Athens virtually destroyed itself in the course and aftermath of the culturally suicidal Peloponnesian War. The rottenness within modern European culture since the beginning of the 18th Century is found, essentially, in the influence of not only Sarpi and his household lackey Galileo, but also their protégés Sir Francis Bacon and Thomas Hobbes, and in such Anglo-Dutch liberals as John Locke, Isaac Newton, Bernard Mandeville, Voltaire, David Hume, François Quesnay, the "curry Wurst" composer Rameau, Adam Smith, Leonhard Euler, Jeremy Bentham, and Immanuel Kant. The specific moral-intellectual rot permeating the cultures of Europe and the U.S.A. today, is rooted in the systemic features common to these creatures of the Seventeenth- and Eighteenth-Century "Enlightenment." The British Empire is the pivotal expression of the Anglo-Dutch variety of the empiricism otherwise known as Romanticism and its outgrowth, existentialism.

London and Fascism

This brings us to that child of the post-World War I Versailles Treaty which is the 1922-1945 reign of fascism on the continent of Europe. The causes of the specific characteristics of that period are rooted in the folly of what was known as the "Versailles" monetary-financial system. Just as a core of the Nazi system was taken into the womb of the Anglo-American victors in World War II, the systemic features of fascism, in its character as a special outgrowth of empiricism, is the root of the especially vicious features of globally extended Anglo-American Liberalism today.

That said: identify fascism summarily, as an outgrowth of the Versailles system, in the following way.

Rather than writing down, as in lawful bankruptcy, the unpayable mass of British, French, and related war-debt accumulated during 1914-1917, Versailles proposed to avoid that remedy (in the main), by the following swindle. Woodrow Wilson's Secretary of State, Lansing, a man designed by disposition to earn much guilt himself, proclaimed, with a cupidity typical of him, that Germany must bear the total guilt for that recent war which had been diligently organized, not by Germans, but by the now-deceased British emperor Edward VII. It might have been suggested that President Woodrow Wilson was so preoccupied with mass-production of uniforms and burnable crosses for his Ku Klux Klan organization at the time, that he made no objection to Lansing's fraud. The relevant majority of the presumably great thinkers assembled as victorious vultures in those post-war proceedings, agreed to this fraud without a serious quibble. John Maynard Keynes did make a noise, but it was only a self-righteous, ineffable footnote on the proceedings. The Germans would pay the reparations needed to feed the bankrupt French and British bankers, out of which sums the British and French would be enabled to pay their war-debts to the eagerly waiting, hungry vultures, the Wall Street financiers.

The hitch, as Keynes noted, is that the whole reparations scheme was a house-of-cards. Simply, as long as Germany was prevented from breaking out of the conditions imposed through Versailles, Germany could never pay the prescribed war-debt. The attempt of Germany to do so, produced the hyperbolic-like spiral of inflation, and then hyperinflation, of 1921-1923. The inability to repeat that kind of bail-out at the close of the decade, led to the fall of the German parliamentary government of Hermann Müller. This become the opportunity for the Bank of England's Montagu Norman, Harriman, et al., to proceed with successive fundings of their intended placement of the Weberian (e.g., "charismatic") psychopath Adolf Hitler, into power in Germany.

From Versailles on, all relevant higher-ranking financial authorities knew, as Keynes did, that the Versailles system based on reparations could not work. It was doomed, from the start, by its own design. Those private financiers and others who mobilized the Synarchist International for the purpose of putting fascist governments into power, already knew the truth about the system at the time of Versailles. They took the view, in effect: "Good! Let it blow up! We will bring in fascist governments everywhere!" The same kind of private financier interest, many of whom are biologically or otherwise direct descendants of the Synarchist financier circles of the Versailles Treaty and its aftermath, have made the same choice, once again, for the world at large, nearly a century later, today. In fact, the determination of the circles of Allen Dulles and James J. Angleton, during and following World War II, to bring about a form of fascist economy, known as a "globalized" world system of "universal fascism," was a continuation of the Nazi utopian goal which Dulles et al. shared with those Nazis whom they had ushered into the postwar American and related allied establishments. That legacy of Allen Dulles, Angleton, the Buckleyites, the late Roy M. Cohn, et al., has been continued by certain Anglo-American factional circles to the present day. The fascist network adopted by Dulles, et al., is the leading terrorist and related menace to civilization today.

Once you know that, you begin to understand the significance of the close connections among 10 Downing Street's "New Labour" Fabians around Blair, Vice-President and international carpet-bagger Dick Cheney, and Tony Blair's fellow-travellers in and around the Democratic Leadership Council in the U.S.A. still today. For the purposes of such fellows, new Nazi-like movements do not have to be built up *de novo*, as if from scratch; they never went away.

As noted and documented earlier, Hitler was put into power by the backing from the collaborators of the Bank of England's Montagu Norman, chiefly financier interests centered in London and New York City. Initially, the intent of those forces in London was to keep the potentially deadly rival, the U.S.A., out of what became World War II. Conditions changed. Edward VIII was dumped, and Churchill led the opposition to those powerful circles in Britain who intended to bring Britain and its navy into the continental fascist scheme to destroy the Soviet Union, and then destroy the naval and related power of the U.S.A. Churchill's motive was simple; he needed no one to teach him affection for fascism, but Churchill represented those who would not make a pact with Europe which would lead to the early dissolution of that British Empire established, in fact, by the 1763 Treaty of Paris. Churchill did not object to fascism; he objected to the development of a Germany-based "universal fascism" order, which would make the British a chess-piece of world politics, rather than the intended Anglo-American "cousins" as the hegemonic player.

Hitler and his regime are now long dead, but, as I have already noted, the surviving core of the Nazi apparatus is now entering its third adult generation through a pact struck between a core of the Nazi apparatus and right-wing Anglo-American circles typified by figures such as Allen Dulles and James J. Angleton. It is still a serious contender within the ranks of the pro-fascist thrust toward world power today. So, the inner core of the fascist rampage of 1922-1945 was tucked within the relevant part of the post-war Anglo-American establishment; and, so, the pestilence which had already created two "world wars," lived on, to plague the world still today.

Unfortunately, with the death of President Roosevelt, the United States under his successor, Harry S Truman, joined with the right-wing of the United Kingdom in making a remarkable right-turn. This right-wing adoption of key elements of the Nazi apparatus, as part of the post-war Anglo-American system, was not mystifying, if one takes into account that the issue which had prompted certain right-wing U.S. financiers and their British cousins to support President Franklin Roosevelt's war-time leadership temporarily, was simply the antipathy of those Brits and the American anglophiles for surrendering what they regarded as their English-speaking union to the yoke of a continental tyrant. As I have stated above, they did not object to Hitler because he was fascist, but because he was a continental figure. In the late Summer of 1944, once the U.S.-led Normandy breakthrough had sealed the fate of Hitler's regime, the British and U.S.A. right-wingers readily, even greedily absorbed that Nazi talent which they regarded as useful to their yearning for world government along the same lines Göring and Company had sought to create international mega-corporations in a globalized economy run by international financier oligarchical syndicates, rather than national capitals.

This right-wing turn was typified by negotiations, by a portion of Anglo-American establishment which brought a core of the Nazi apparatus, around such figures as Hjalmar Schacht, Otto Skorzeny, Schellenberg, Wolf, and the fascist Synarchist International's financier network, into the post-war Anglo-American system, including the functions of NATO. The collaboration between those Nazi and Anglo-American circles, produced its so-called "utopian" faction of strategic policy-shaping of the post-war period to date. This faction, which relied significantly on using complicit Franco's fascist Spain for planting, and continued support, of Nazi influences into post-war Central and South America, was defined not only by an initial commitment to so-called "preventive warfare" against the Soviet Union, but by the dominant role of Bertrand Russell and his collaborators in defining a global policy of "world government won through the terror of nuclear-fission weaponry," as the needless nuclear bombing of the civilian populations of Hiroshima and Nagasaki attests. The launching of the doctrine of "world government preventive nuclear war," by the British Fabian Society's Mephistophelean Bertrand Russell, combined with the needless nuclear bombing of the civilian populations of Hiroshima and Nagasaki, defined the launching of the utopian right-wing doctrine of the nuclear right-wing factions in the U.S., Britain, and NATO, down to the present day.

This nuclear policy defines that "utopian" faction to which President Dwight Eisenhower referred as a "military-industrial complex," the banker-run complex of that time, of which more decadent Vice-President Cheney and his neoconservatives, like the similarly morally and intellectually decayed current incumbents of 10 Downing Street, are representative today.

Truman's folly in adopting Bertrand Russell's, and Winston Churchill's "utopian" orientation toward "preventive nuclear war" against the Soviet Union, led to the quagmire of the U.S. war in Korea, and the stunning revelation that the Soviet Union had achieved priority in development and successful testing of a deployable thermonuclear-fusion weapon. This situation led to Truman's retirement and the Eisenhower alternative. "Preventive nuclear war" gave way. However, "preventive nuclear war" returned, during Dick Cheney's stint as Secretary of Defense, under President George H.W. Bush, Sr. At that time, Cheney et al. saw the collapse of the Soviet Union's power as the opportunity to revive a "preventive nuclear war" doctrine. Now, with the pathetic son of the father serving as resident dummy in the White House, George Shultz's retained ventriloquists, Cheney, neo-Wellsian Condoleezza Rice, et al., are putting the evil Mr. Cheney's nuclear madness into operation—unless they are prevented by a U.S. suddenly come back to its senses, now.

In the meantime, back during the 1950s, the seed of what Cheney represents today, was planted with the consolidation of Soviet General Secretary Khrushchev's position as Stalin's successor. Khrushchev, in concert with Russell, the latter the original architect of the doctrine of imperial world government through preventive nuclear war, put on the table what was to become known as "mutual and assured thermonuclear destruction," otherwise known as "detente." The missile-crisis of 1962 was an expression of that Russell-Khrushchev relationship. With the collapse of Soviet power during the 1989-1992 interval, Cheney et al. shifted from "detente," back to that pushing for preventive nuclear war which remains Cheney's policy, as Vice-President, today.

So, in that way, this Anglo-American-based outgrowth of the fascist overlordship of western and central continental Europe during the 1922-1945 interval, became known as the military utopianism reflected in the brutish moral criminality and barefaced lying of Vice-President Dick Cheney and his 10 Downing Street Fabian cronies today.

To understand this utopianism in a deeper, more effective way, we must recognize it as essentially the creation of two Fabian Society fathers, the utopian H.G. Wells of **The Open Conspiracy** notoriety, and Bertrand Russell's leading role in designing and promoting the doctrine of "world government through (perpetual) preventive nuclear warfare."

The Russell doctrine was already being put through mass-rehearsals, prior to Hiroshima, by the Joseph de Maistre-style of Churchill-Lindemann doctrine of mass-murder of civilian populations, through creating fire-storm holocausts against the large non-military targets in Germany. The attempted British fire-storm in Berlin did not succeed, because the relevant Berlin avenues were too wide for the scheme to succeed; it was intended, for a while, to use the U.S. nuclear weapons on Berlin; but, the bomb was not ready for that use at the time it might have been so used. Instead, the Truman Administration consoled itself with the strategically counterproductive fire-bombing of the civilian population of Tokyo, and President Truman's utterly useless, militarily, nuclear bombing of Hiroshima and Nagasaki.

1.2 When I Came on Stage

I became, suddenly, a political figure on the world stage during Aug. 15-30, 1971. There were three factors involved in bringing this about.

The first factor, was simply factual. I was the only known economist of note who had accurately forecast publicly that kind of developments, and their outcome, developments which had been set into motion by policies responsible for a series of grave monetary crises during the 1967-1971 interval. Every notable economics textbook, its author, and its forecasts were shown, suddenly and in the most undeniable way, that my forecast had not only been accurate; but, more important, the only competent *method* of forecasting which was then visible on the world stage. My success on this occasion had international reverberations. Fortunately, but I think not accidentally, I have never spoiled that professional record as an economist during the decades since.

The second factor was an issue of the economic profession's prevalent range of doctrines. Since my humiliating defeat of Keynesian Professor Abba Lerner, chosen to challenge me on behalf of the profession in a celebrated, late 1971 debate, no economist opposed to my views has ever dared to challenge me in open classical debate format on economic and related policy-

matters since. Usually, an outpouring of irrelevant, lying defamation is employed as a way of fending off the challenge to debate some terrified target of my challenge to such an encounter.

The third factor was political. I had warned that were the radical, anti-Franklin Roosevelt policy-changes in economic policy not reversed, the world was headed toward the only kind of regime which coincided with the effects of Nixon's policy: fascism, worldwide.

One point of explanation of my most unusual successes in this and related domains, should be made clear as an integral feature of the method which permeates the subsuming subject of this report as a whole.

More significant than all other factors responsible for the customary incompetence of economists and others posing as long-range forecasters, is the myth of the existence of an absolute, "the inevitable event." Whenever someone claims to have foreseen some event which he, or she claims to been an unconditionally pre-determined inevitability, that forecaster is self-exposed as intrinsically incompetent in that sort of work. As the success of Frederick the Great against the Austrians at Leuthen attests—or the defeat of both Napoleon Bonaparte's and his successor Hitler's invasion of Russia—the commander who saw the available choice of flanking action which another had overlooked, often secured victory precisely because his opponent had planned an "inevitable" victory. There are no unconditional, monotonic inevitabilities of specific events in the universe. What is "unconditional" is the imminence of a limited array of critical choices. In the case of the present world monetary-financial collapse, the characteristic feature of the overall situation, is a narrowing of the margin of those choices which might be considered acceptable to one or another of the relevant parties.

Take the case of the presently looming threat of rather immediate collapse into a general, global breakdown-crisis, of the world's present monetary-financial system. All of the choices adopted by leading relevant authorities, thus far, in the attempt to postpone the point of general collapse of that system, have the following net effect.

The adoption of a system of "post-industrial" economy by the U.S.A., Britain, and others, was associated with a second rule of thumb, radically extended forms of "free trade." The growth of "outsourcing" through the means of a "floating-exchange-rate" monetary system, over an initial period 1971-1982, created the preconditions for accelerated looting of weaker na-

"During the second half of 1977, I was informed of the fight over the development of 'new physical principles' ongoing within the Pentagon. I took the side of the proponents of 'new physical principles,' but I knew that . . . without a general change in strategic doctrine, 'new physical principles' could be degraded into the character of a technological gimmick." The LaRouche/Reagan SDI developed new x-ray lasers and telescopes (below), and powerful infrared sensors with space and Earth uses (left).

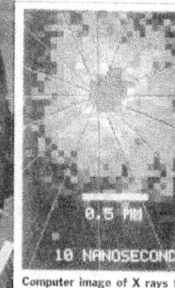

Computer image of X rays from 10 trillion-watt generator, left, which powers experimental laser

tions. This, in turn, paved the way for "outsourcing," and for the radical extreme of "outsourcing," which Ross Perot, in 1992, described as "that great sucking sound." The result was the collapsing of higher-price capital investment and productive employment in the U.S.A., the U.K., and other more industrialized nations, through aid of a low-wage policy for the new exporting nations, which latter was an echo of the same form of primitive capital accumulation practiced by Hermann Göring's steering of the practices of the Nazi mega-cartels employing forced and concentration-camp labor.

As a result, the physical-capital ratios, per capita and per square-kilometer, of most of the world, including a massive looting and destruction of the single greatest, 1989-2004 part of this worldwide destruction, the former Soviet Union, has reduced the net physical-capital of the world, while hyperinflationary methods, especially the "John Law"-style financial-derivatives innovations launched by U.S. Federal Reserve Chairman Alan Greenspan, have unleashed what is, in fact, the greatest hyperinflationary bubble in history, a bubble more than ready to be popped now.

During the course of this time, especially since the oncoming systemic collapse of the world system was clearly visible, in 1987, the highest-ranking fools of the world, and others, have often congratulated themselves on their cleverness in postponing the already ripe collapse, by intrinsically hyperinflationary methods which made the next crisis more deadly than the preceding

ones. Witness: the outsourcing bubble ("great sucking sound") which Vice-President Al Gore pushed. Witness: the IT bubble, financed by Alan Greenspan's lunacy, and premised on the terror of a touted collapse of the world on Jan. 1, 2000. Witness: the British and Greenspan's lunatic mortgage-backed-securities bubble. Witness: the Fall 1998 decision to use a massive outpouring of a hyperinflationary "wall of money," in the attempt to ensure that the general collapse would occur under President Clinton's successor; thus, the punishment so implicitly intended for Gore, which fell actually upon a Bush who successfully snatched the brass ring of folly from the foolish fingers of rival Gore.

So, over the entire period, beginning with Aug. 15, 1971, the Anglo-American hegemons have led the world in general, step by step along the road toward ultimate doom. At each critical point, there were alternatives. The only good alternative, was to scrap the radical change in economic policy which had been launched, in the wake of the Kennedy assassination, by the pro-utopian faction. The second class of alternatives, which represented no more than medium-term, or even short-term stop-gap measures, like that taken by President Clinton in the last quarter of 1998, always led to a worse threat of collapse than the preceding charlatan's nostrum.

Through all of this, there was a different sort of available choice. Scrap the system these charlatans were defending, and return to the proven principles of the Roosevelt recovery which had carried the United States and others, from March 1933 through the death of President Kennedy. Those geniuses were fleeing, in fact, toward their legendary meeting with doom, in Samara.

A concise summary of the way I foresaw the end toward which my rival economists were misleading their clients, runs as follows.

The mathematical-physical paradigm for the doom now descending upon the present world monetary-financial system, is Bernhard Riemann's famous analysis of the way in which a sonic shock-wave is generated, and also transcended. The relevant comparison is as follows.

What we are facing is not a recession, or cyclical depression. We are now faced with a systemic disintegration of that existing system. The only escape to safety, is by dumping that system, in favor of a return to a type of new system not inconsistent with the recovery methods which President Franklin Roosevelt applied to both the U.S. economic recovery, and the extension of that to rebuilding a war-shattered world—the original, Roosevelt-defined, Bretton Woods system. The operation to be performed is comparable to the achievement of "breaking the sound barrier" as the latter was originally defined by Riemann. The possibility of survival under these conditions, depends upon applying the lessons of FDR's successes to the process of placing the existing system into receivership by sovereign governments, for government-supervised reorganization in bankruptcy under conditions of a government-credit-launched general economic recovery.

The "sound barrier" in this case is not a fixed value, but a relative one. The "sound barrier" analogue, against which the hyperinflationary surge of monetary-financial aggregate is being thrown, is determined by a ratio of the rate of increase of such aggregate, relative to the rate of contraction of real physical assets, per capita and per square kilometer. The kind of mathematical function so described may be viewed, in first approximation, as hyperbolic.[11] In this case, the increase of the financial-monetary aggregate is tied to a function of decline of net physical output per capita and per square kilometer. This is the case because the increase of credit

to feed the financial-monetary bubble, depends upon what is termed "primitive (e.g., parasitical) capital accumulation" against the physical basis. The result is an apparent increase of the steepness of the hyperbolic curve of financial-monetary aggregate, relative to each increment in of time. Time itself is relative, in this case. The rate at which the economy is looted to prevent it from collapse, determines the relative time expressed by the function overall.

When the steepness of the hyperbolic-like curve approaches "straight up," an absolute limit for the system has been approached very nearly. In that interval, which expresses itself with increasingly wild turbulence, the boundary layer reflecting the outer limit of the existence of the world monetary-financial system has been reached.

But even at the point, there is an option. Change the system, as I have proposed consistently over about four decades. It is the unwillingness of the relevant parties to consider changing the system itself, as I have proposed, which is the only reason they have to fear what they might regard as the inevitable doom of the world-system. Therefore, they fear and hate me, because my existence, by emphasizing that the collapse of the world economy is by no means inevitable, implicitly threatens the world they wish to have. As empiricist James Clerk Maxwell explained his fraudulent refusal to acknowledge his borrowings from the discoveries of Gauss, Weber, and Riemann, Maxwell and his British colleagues had wittingly refused to acknowledge the existence of "any geometries but our own."

Finally, on this matter of "inevitability." The rationale usually employed in a kind of formalist's defense of the notion of inevitability, is the same type of argument central to the underlying folly of all Aristotelian thinking, and also of the neo-Aristotelian modes known as empiricism, positivism, and existentialism. The problem is typified in the writings of Kepler, such as his **The New Astronomy**, in Kepler's focus on the fraud, in astronomy, by the Aristotelian Claudius Ptolemy and the pro-Aristotelian follies of Copernicus and Tycho Brahe. This is otherwise to be recognized, to the same net effect, as the pathologically anti-Promethean ideology of the Delphi cult, and the Eleatics, Sophists, Aristotelians, and empiricists generally. The core of the aspect of that issue which is of relevance in the present immediate context of the principles of forecasting, is expressed by the difference between the concept of "power," by pre-Aristotelian Classical Greek science,

---

11. Actually, the comparison to geometric determination of the catenary function, as Leibniz and Bernouilli defined this in connection with Leibniz's principle of universal physical least-action, were more appropriate. For present purposes of illustration, the notion of the lower-power hyperbolic function will be adequate.

and Aristotle's proposed substitute for "power," "energy." Energy is an effect; power is the action whose footprint may often be termed "energy."

When we recognize that a failed self-esteemed forecaster thinks in terms of statistical or kindred extrapolations from observed effects, to the effect of assuming that an adduced pattern of effects is the motive for the subsequent outcome, we have put our finger on the deepest source of that forecaster's incompetence.

The essential distinction of man from the beast, is the individual human mind's sovereign power of cognitive insight, a power corresponding exactly to Plato's principle of hypothesis. The discovery of a previously unknown physical principle, by the Platonic method of hypothesis, equips us with efficient knowledge of some otherwise invisible, but already efficiently existing principle of the universe, a principle which existed implicitly in the entire scope of Creation itself. The adoption of that discovered principle, when practiced by man, is a power of man to change the universe.

The essential issue of the history of science, LaRouche insists, is the principle of Socratic hypothesis brought to life in the dialogues of Plato (above), by which mankind discovers what can not be sensed directly; and the empiricism introduced to Europe by Venice's Paolo Sarpi (right). "Empiricism is a modern echo of the ruinous reign of sophistry by which Athens virtually destroyed itself."

The very existence of man as a distinct species, resides entirely in that point I have just summarized. It is the motivating intent to cause a form of action, which expresses a discovered universal physical principle, which is the sole cause for the continued existence of the human species. Change, so defined, is the only form of existence actually known to mankind. Thus the passion to change the universe, rather than following intellectually and morally rotten Rome in preferring the illusion of fixed permanent laws of a mythical universe—the Aristotelian or comparable source of that deadly delusion which is to be recognized in the form of belief in inevitable outcomes.

This was the characteristic principle of evil ruling Rome; this was the utopia envisaged by Diocletian. This is the evil represented by the idea of a perpetual British empire, as by Lord Shelburne's crew, or a "Thousand-Year Reich," or the almost or actually Satanic belief in submission to a pre-fixed state of nature,

as by the mentally and morally crippled "greenie." The search for a permanent ordering of the universe is an impulse which cripples its believer, intellectually and morally. At its least worst, it renders the victim of such a delusion psycho-sexually impotent. As a policy which the victim of such a delusion seeks to impose upon others, or society generally, it is the evil from which empires and fascism like Hitler's and Michael Ledeen's spread.

The economists whose wrath I have thus requickened by these remarks, represent a lackey-like dedication to fostering their careers in service to their actual or would-be master. They are apologists for their master, even comparable to parish priests of a Satanic-like cult. They wish to keep the world within the bounds of their master's pleasure. They are psycho-sexually inert, as faithful harem eunuchs are, to the effect of their seeking to assure only inevitably predetermined outcomes, because they have no reason to exist, but to defend their masters' delusions against all disturbing noises. They are stupid, because, for that reason, they wish to appear stupid.

Why My Enemies Feared My Superiority

As official documents, later released, attest, during 1973 the national Federal Bureau of Investigation (FBI) was engaged, through its assets in the leadership of the Communist Party U.S.A., in a plan to bring about my personal elimination. Our detection of that operation, during December 1973, led to the abortion of actual Communist Party deployments coinciding with what the later released official FBI internal document confirmed. The Loudoun County, Virginia events of October 6-7, 1986 and the Alexandria trial of 1988, are to be understood as essentially a continuation of a persisting pattern of similar intention and character over that period, extending to London's 10 Downing Street-based, Cheney-linked, operations in Europe and elsewhere, today.

The aversive operations of kindred nature from sundry agencies and the financier oligarchy-controlled press, were escalated by several crucial features of my 1976 U.S. Presidential campaign, which was effectively a campaign against Henry A. Kissinger's utopian successor, Trilateral Commission founder and presumptive National Security Advisor Zbigniew Brzezinski. Brzezinski, obviously, was not pleased by my tampering with the intended success of several of his nastier ventures. The reaction zoomed with the SDI campaign, lost some of its vigor with my imprisonment, but erupted into successive escalations in 1996, the 2000 Democratic Presidential campaign, and my critical interventions into the worsening U.S. situation under the current President. The pattern here is not a succession of events, but, rather a continuing process which generates a succession of discrete effects. I illustrate the process by identifying a few of its exemplary effects.

My development of the proposal which President Reagan named the SDI, began with my reaction to a discovery of a document which chanced to fall into my hands during the 1976 Presidential campaign. That information became the most widely recognized feature of my 1976 Presidential campaign, and the subject of an election-eve, nationwide TV broadcast that year. For that alone, some of the establishment have never forgiven me to the present day.

During the 1975-1976 run-up to Zbigniew Brzezinski's replacing what had been his former Harvard bedfellow, under "house mother" Professor William Yandell Elliott, Henry A. Kissinger's position as National Security Advisor,[12] I chanced upon what is fairly termed "hot and solid evidence," that a section of the proposed Carter Administration—a section associated with utopian J. Rodney Schlesinger—was tinkering with an intention to stage what would readily become a nuclear standoff with the Soviet Union. Therefore, my 1976 U.S. Presidential candidacy featured my sounding the alarm against this feature of the incoming Brzezinski Administration's schemes. That warning succeeded in its purpose; there were no more such squeaks about "present danger" from Schlesinger's niche in the Brzezinski cabal during President Carter's term. Nonetheless, I had learned the lesson from that experience; the United States must find a science-aided alternative to the dead-end game of "Peace through Mutual Thermonuclear Terror."

My ability to turn an accumulation of scattered scientific and related facts into a strategic doctrine, depended upon a feature of my knowledge which lay outside the bounds of the generally accepted notions of the science-classroom. I have tended to rely, pedagogically, more and more on what I describe as "the fishbowl syndrome" to portray to others the characteristic way in which cultures tend to cling, stubbornly, to systemic delusions which tend to ensure a self-inflicted downfall or severe injury of an entire nation, an entire culture.

The post-1954 effort to restructure the entire cultures of Europe and the Americas, in particular, around development of what came to be known as "detente," is an example of that sort of systemic pathology. The Kissinger and Brzezinski phases of this variety of utopian strategic doctrine, was the pathology which I addressed in my design for an alternative to this utopian nightmare, an alternative expressed in the form of what became known as a "Strategic Defense Initiative."

What became known as "SDI," at least in the way I defined it, was based on an understanding of the relevant aspects of the prevalent "fishbowl syndrome" of that time. The solution for the challenge so defined could not have been developed into what became

---

12. Elliott, noted as an American agent of British intelligence influence, was a prominent member of a right-wing association, with Fabian connections, known as the Nashville Agrarians. That association represented the tradition of the Tennessee founders of the original Ku Klux Klan. Den mother Elliott's charges in his Harvard department of government, where Kissinger was reared, have been more or less consistently agents of the so-called "utopian" (i.e., "universal fascist," Schacht) faction in U.S. military affairs to the present day.

known as SDI, except from the standpoint which I had contributed to the founding and developing of the FEF.

About the same time I acquired the evidence of the nuclear-war-like intentions of Trilateral Commission circles associated with James Rodney Schlesinger, a fight had already broken out within the Defense Department over the issue of development of what the diplomatic lexicon identifies as "new physical principles" of defense against nuclear-armed intercontinental missiles. In the process, the then-current head of the Defense Intelligence Agency, Lt.-General Daniel P. Graham, was a typical, fanatical opponent of such development. Graham was later to become a leading, rather savage 1982-83 opponent of both me and Dr. Edward Teller on this issue. Graham demanded, as in his 1982 campaign for a kookish scheme called "High Frontier," that missile defense be limited to systems which had already, correctly been defined as obsolete back during the early 1960s.

During the second half of 1977, I was informed of the fight over the development of "new physical principles" ongoing within the Pentagon. I took the side of the proponents of "new physical principles," but I knew that those boosting the use of these principles there had not yet grasped the deeper implications of what they were supporting. In response, I recognized that without a general change in strategic doctrine, "new physical principles" could be degraded into the character of a technological gimmick. I concentrated on developing the needed doctrine, the doctrine which became known later, as SDI.

Before continuing with the process leading to the most recent reaction of the commitment to preventive nuclear war by Cheney et al., we must lay the groundwork with a look at those processes of the human mind which permitted modern society to drive into the kind of lunacy which Cheney merely typifies today.

These developments have divided the military professionals and related political circles of the U.S.A. between two factions, the sane (the "traditionalists" typified by Generals of the Armies MacArthur and Eisenhower) and the lunatic "utopians," typified by the followers of Churchill, Lindemann, Bertrand Russell, and RAND warrior clans, et al. The latter set of dangerous lunatics are to be diagnosed as a special case of what I have found it convenient to describe as a typical "fishbowl mentality."

Since I am, as I have qualified this, a Promethean, I do not seek to fix hopelessly dysfunctional systems; I save my efforts to the purpose of making the necessary change in the system. My advantage, in crafting the original design for the policy which became known as the original, March 23, 1983 doctrine of SDI, differed from all others: In the sense that I used the idea of the implications of "new physical principles," to a strategic political end, a change in the world political system, as the basis for the employment of relevant scientific-technological and related military-systems changes in the strategic configuration which had to be revolutionized. In effect, all of this, combined, was a fresh application of the same principle, applied to the 1945-1983 strategic conflict, which Cardinal Mazarin, et al., had applied, in the Treaty of Westphalia, to bring the Thirty Years War of 1618-1648 to a peaceful conclusion.

The objective of modern warfare is its unavoidable function as the securing of a peace which could be achieved in no other way. Thus, the design of forces, weapons-systems, and their applications must be designed accordingly. To achieve that result, we must start backwards in time, from the peace sought, to the selection of the means needed to bring that about.

Therefore, the crucial point of reference by me, to the Soviet side of the equation, was the fact that the Soviet military-scientific establishment could produce what were, under the circumstances on their side, relative miracles of applied science; whereas, the performance of the civilian side of the economy, frankly, stunk, as most learned relevant Soviet publications acknowledged to the degree political discretion permitted. The peace-making objective for the U.S.A., must therefore focus on that irony of the situation. That was my approach in 1982-1983, when I conducted an authorized back-channel dialogue with the Soviet government's representative on behalf of President Reagan's National Security Council.

The U.S. approach to defense, at that time, was based largely on technologically obsolescent junk produced by Wall Street's favorite military contractors. Gen. Daniel Graham's "High Frontier"—not merely "high," but virtually psychedelic—reflected that folly. The object must be to shift the military-hardware parameters to a *long-term agreement* on a shift from Bertrand Russell-style, obsolete weapons of mutually assured destruction, to higher order technologies which could become the weapons for escaping that deadly paradox, but, *but, but* would provide a science-driver up shift of the economies participating in the agreement. This up shift must occur in a way consistent with the principle of "the advantage of the other" which produced the miraculous end of a virtual dark age of religious warfare, in the 1648 Treaty of Westphalia.

My view had a certain novelty, but it was completely consistent with the principles of nation-building-based strategic defense which had been developed by Lazare Carnot, Gerhard Scharnhorst, and our own science-engineering-based military professionals, through the service of Generals of the Armies MacArthur and Eisenhower. It was the Christian principle, of give your ostensible adversary bread in exchange for a stone.

This traditionalist implication of my design was widely recognized and supported among leading military-professional and related circles in Europe and elsewhere. That very fact, however, points to the reasons I was so bitterly hated for my role in the matter of SDI. I was threatening to take away the cookies of the fascist babies, merely typified by Vice-President Cheney, buzzards who had their gizzards set for a utopian enterprise of world government achieved through nuclear terror. Hence, the cry: "Eliminate him!"

1.3 'The Fishbowl Syndrome'

By "fishbowl" I mean the a state of mind in which the individual's view of the universe is viciously out of physical, cause-effect correspondence with that real universe in which he is engaged in reciprocal action.

What is recognizable as the "reductionist" form of belief, represents a wide variety of specific sets of belief, which all together, while otherwise differing among themselves, are mental disorders of a common type, mental disorders which, even when otherwise specifically distinct from one another, share a common, specific quality of flawed characteristics. The more readily understandable expressions of such mental disorders, are encountered in the influence of the forms of reductionist pathologies encountered in physical science, but, most emphatically, within the domain of mathematics. In modern European cultures, the bulk of these pathologies afflicting mathematical science are traced, as it is said, "hereditarily," from an overlap of currents rooted in Aristotelianism and empiricism. Today, the best opportunity to gain an overview of the functional characteristics of reductionist disorders in the practice of physical science, is the revolutionary work of Bernhard Riemann

The truth is, that the essential difference which separates all men and women absolutely, and equally, from all other living species, is the Platonic principle of Socratic hypothesis. Man is able to see, and to prove the existence of objects called "universal physical principles," which can not be seen as objects of sense-perception. As man accumulates knowledge and mastery of these universal principles, which pre-Euclidean Greek science knew as "powers" (i.e., *dynamis*), mankind's power in, and over the universe is increased to such effects as increasing society's potential relative population-density, as measurable per-capita and per-square-kilometer of the Earth's surface.

Thus, the mind of the human individual expresses a power which is generated for action within the mental processes of a living person, but which can not be identified as a product of the individual's biology. There is no basis for arbitrary, or otherwise irrational speculation in this distinction. The universe, as recognized by ancient Classical Greek scientists and, in a notable modern case, V.I. Vernadsky, is a manifold of three multiply-connected phase-spaces, which latter we distinguish experimentally as the *abiotic*, the *living*, and, lastly, what is termed the *noëtic*, or *cognitive*. The point to be emphasized, is that the human individual's acquisition of efficient knowledge of a discovered, experimentally validated, universal physical principle expresses the active presence of a fully efficient universal phase-space, a phase space which requires an experimental method distinct from the methods sufficient for either abiotic phase-space, or a merely living phase-space.

This is the matter of the fraudulent argument which Carl Gauss refuted in his 1799 attack on the hoax of Euler, Lagrange, et al.

Modern studies of the astronomical characteristics of Egyptian astronomy from before the erection of the great pyramids, confirmed the Greek accounts, as by Plato and others, that the notably leading elements of Greek scientific culture came from Egypt. This was expressed by that Pythagorean notion of "spherics," which served as the basis for pre-Aristotelian, and pre-Euclidean geometry. Four most elementary features of the Pythagorean science of Plato et al., are the construction of the doubling of the line, the construction of the doubling of the square, the construction of the doubling of the cube, and the Platonic solids. The first three of these four, are the points of reference employed by Gauss to show the fraudulent character of those notions

Utopian madmen of the "MAD" Doctrine in the 1960s and 1970s: Henry Kissinger (with patron David Rockefeller, left) and Zbigniew Brzezinski when he controlled the Jimmy Carter White House. "The Kissinger and Brzezinski phases of this variety of utopian strategic doctrine, was the pathology which I addressed in my design for an alternative to this utopian nightmare, an alternative expressed in the form of what became known as a 'Strategic Defense Initiative.'"

of a fundamental theorem of algebra associated with d'Alembert, Euler, and Lagrange. The action which generates each those three constructions is a *power* as the Pythagoreans and Plato define the meaning of *power* (Gr.: *dynamis*). The doubling of the cube is the simplest and clearest representation of the principle underlying all cases, as the relevant problem was posed by Cardan to his successors. Thus, Gauss's 1799 argument against Euler and Lagrange, implicitly defines the physical significance of the complex domain underlying the general notion of a fundamental theorem of algebra.

These discoveries of universal physical principle, are not merely methods of mathematical description, as if at the blackboard. They represent the discovery, and wielding, by man, of efficiently acting universal physical principles which existed before man's acquaintance with their existence. The principle of experimental proof signifies man's demonstration of his ability to secure willful control over the use of that principle, that in ways which may change the way in which the universe unfolds from that point on. That is to say, that, as Vernadsky emphasized, just as the acting principle of life works in a way which is external to the abiotic processes of Earth, to generate the change known as the

transformation of the ostensibly abiotic planet into a Biosphere, man's willful use of discovered universal physical principles, superimposes those qualitative changes which, cumulatively, transform the planet from a Biosphere to define the Noösphere. *A true discovery of any universal physical principle, is a grasp of the power to make a willful change in the ordering of the universe.* The universal physical principle discovered, existed, and functioned in the universe before man first discovered it. Nonetheless, when man not only discovers, but deploys such a principle, man's willful action in using that principle changes the universe. Hence, such discoveries are to be recognizing as acting "powers" for changing the world, in the sense of that usage by pre-Euclidean Greeks such as the Pythagoreans, Heraclitus, and Plato.

In physical science, "power," so defined as the desired alternative to the term of superstition named "energy," means either a power by which we willfully change the universe, or a power which bounds the pathway of action of a principle which we are willfully deploying. This notion, and the distinctions it incorporates, have been made qualitatively clearer by the original discoveries of Bernard Riemann.

Modern insight into this feature of universal physical science as such, depends upon the revolutionary discovery central to Bernhard Riemann's 1854 habilitation dissertation. This work freed science from all remaining obligation to believe in such "fishbowl"-like substitutes for knowledge as the definitions, axioms, and postulates of a Euclidean deductive system. In place of so-called "self-evident," *a priori* assumptions, competent science now declares that we know nothing except what we know as a relatively unique quality of experimental proof of some Platonic form of hypothesis which serves us efficiently as a man-discovered universal physical principle. Henceforth, from that, man is freed by Riemann's demonstration, beginning his celebrated, 1854 habilitation dissertation, from all definitions, axioms, and postulates, and the kinds of deductive method associated with them.

Not only are the *a priori* kinds of definitions, axioms, and postulates false, inherently. The acceptance of such a set of beliefs corrupts the mind of the duped believer, to the effect of erecting a mental barrier, within which false universe, the individual's and society's ability to act is self-confined, as we may say of a pet fish ostensibly content to continue swimming out his life within a fishbowl.

Take the example of a currently widespread, popular delusion, the notion of a physical principle of "free trade," as a relevant illustrative case in point.

From the standpoint of physical reality, rather than financial-accounting mythologies, the term "profit" has no rational meaning, except as indicating an anti-entropic form of action which generates more power than is required to generate it. This physical definition of profit may be restated as the portion of the total physical output, when that is expressed in the form of power, which must be allotted, beyond maintaining the existence of the producer and the means the producer employs, to produce the relevant total outcome.

In a modern physical economy, three features of this process are outstanding. The replacement of the family which provided the producer an equal or better functional condition. The replacement of the means of production used, in an equal or better function condition. The replacement of the infrastructure of society, on which the equal or better existence of that society and its means of production depend.

However, in the practice of "free trade," the following insanity occurs.

The price of goods is reduced, by lowering the quality of the labor employed. The price of goods is reduced, by cannibalizing the existing physical capital. The price of goods is reduced, temporarily, by depletion of the pre-existing natural conditions and standard of life, up to the point of a general state of at least relative collapse of the system.

In the unfortunate case, that a nation, or nations are deluded into believing that "free trade's" changes must necessarily lead to an improvement: On principle, the point at which the depletion of society by cannibalizing populations, means of production, and infrastructure (including nature itself), will approach the condition of a breakdown of the system, defines a boundary of that foolish society's continued existence in that form. That defines a "fishbowl." Either the system is reformed, to eliminate the "free trade" factor, or the society collapses. "Get out of the fishbowl, or die."

Reliance on "free trade" as the factor of social practice whose application must be perfected, as in the case of so-called "globalization" versions of the "free trade" cult today, tends to eliminate all factors of economic-policy-directed activity which might be seen by relevant "free trade" ideological fanatics as exceptions to the perfected, universal application of the "free trade" rule. This is precisely the effect which has been seen as a trend in the Americas and Europe during the post-1987 interval. This trend is the underlying cause of the onrushing general breakdown of the present, U.S.-Britain-dominated, financial-derivatives-rotted-out, world monetary-financial system. So, our incumbent U.S. President, cap-and-bells aroused, hears that "free trade's" effects are ruining the economy; "That means we need a heavier dose of free trade," he replies.

Look at the lunatic's "fishbowl" of "I believe in free trade," as it has shaped the devolution of the U.S. political-economic system since the aftermath of the assassination of President John F. Kennedy by the Nazi-linked interests which the cats, Allen Dulles and James J. Angleton dragged in from their Nazi recruits in Germany, François Genoud's Switzerland, and northern Italy, once President Franklin Roosevelt had died.

There were important flaws in post-Franklin Roosevelt monetary, economic, and foreign policies prior to the removal of the "military-industrial-complex's" obstacle, Kennedy. However, those new policies which have led into the U.S. economic disasters of the past forty years, were not a product of the FDR legacy which persisted among the economic policies of the 1933-1963 interval. The presently onrushing collapse of the end-phase of the post-Kennedy world monetary-financial system, is the product of an intention to bring about what Henry Kissinger crony, and wild-eyed right-wing utopian Michael Ledeen, has praised as a "universal fascist" mode of imperial world government.

As I have summarized this point, respecting "fishbowl" ideologies, in sundry earlier locations, we have the following.

Riemann freed mathematical physics from the grip of so-called "self-evident," *a priori* definitions, axioms, and postulates. After that, not only are they no longer necessary; the continued reliance on such assumptions is specifically pathological in nature, and in ultimate consequences. Assumptions of that type fall among, chiefly, three general classes. A.) A type of assumption which has at least an experimentally grounded, shadowy correspondence to the existence of a lurking principle. B.) A type of assumption, such as "free trade," which is perniciously false. C.) A failure to keep an active sort of open-mindedness about the existence of actual universal principles beyond present knowledge.

This composition of the essentially reductionist form of axiomatic and kindred assumptions, is otherwise flawed by the general view that these assumptions, the best or worst of them, can be treated as independently axiomatic factors, rather than as part of a Riemannian form of multiply-connected array. Since this may appear strange to those lacking experience on this ground, I must explain this point.

In a Riemannian physical geometry, the only allowed assumptions of an axiomatic implication, are discovered hypotheses which have been validated, as universal physical or subsumed principles, by a quality of experiment which is designated as "unique": an experiment which, by its nature, shows the principle to be not only valid experimentally, but absolutely, or relatively universal. No other form or quality of assumption is allowed as equivalent to one of axiomatic universality.

That does mean that Euclidean space and time (and the Cartesian outgrowth of that delusion) are to be banned from present and future science. The remedy is elementary: return to the pre-Euclidean notion of *spherics* which the Pythagoreans and Plato adopted from the methods of Egyptian spherical astronomy. All of the great achievements of European science have been rooted in the notions of a physical, rather than formally abstract geometry, as typified by the root of competent modern science in the work of the followers of Thales, the Pythagoreans, and Plato.

The trouble with *a priori* assumptions, even those which are not malicious, is that they incorporate a margin of a polluting kind of practical error, that as a hereditary feature of the practice of that belief. So, a culture which has adopted even not terribly bad working assumptions, in place of actually universal physical principles, must tend to collapse in the longer term, because of the cumulative effect of the margin of error in a practical assumption.

The notion of truth, in the strictly higher sense, presumes a practical correspondence of the image of the universe in the mind of the actor (an actor such as a society), and the real universe. Therefore, we must be occupied by attention to those *systemic* features of a set of axiomatic-like beliefs which are in contradiction to the way in which the universe actually works. By *systemic*, we should intend to point toward a stubbornly vicious practical conflict between the consequences of an axiomatic quality of decision-making, and the assumed consequences. A case in point, is the way in which lunatic belief in "free trade" has played a leading role as a systemic feature of the forty-year decline of the U.S. economy, from the world's leading producer nation, to the pile of post-industrial garbage which the economy has become today.

A state of mind which is both relatively free of false axiomatic assumptions, and also actively seeking new, positive improvements in its roster of assumptions, is a truthful mind. A contrary opinion, is a man progressing, step by step, toward doom. The doom is the fruit of the lie. Thus, the imagined intention of strolling toward paradise, turns out, in the end, to be a descent into Hell. That is the "fishbowl" of paranoia which has come to dominate the U.S.A. under the temporary reign of the soon-to-retire Baby Boomer generation today.

2. Economy and Science

The theme of this report so far has been, that the present world monetary-financial system is presently in the terminal, breakdown phase of a general collapse. The end of the world is by no means inevitable on this account; but there is, in fact, no possible way in which that present system could be revived, as if in something resembling its present form. The present onrush of that

The most widespread symptom of disease of empiricism: the "fishbowl syndrome," by which individuals, populations, or national leaderships insist that their accustomed fishbowl of events and axioms is the only world, and swim in its same small circles even when it is "dumped." Here, the cartoonist's appropriate example is Alan "Greenspin."

general economic collapse, combined with the intersecting onrush toward an ultimately global form of generalized asymmetric warfare, is the principal feature of the present world crisis-situation. Only the replacement of the present monetary-financial system by a new one, a new one organized through the putting of the old into government receivership for reorganization, represents a feasible alternative to onrushing doom.

In the meantime, as noted above, I am not only the most successful long-range forecaster of recent decades, but perhaps the only person presently living who has an at least adequate comprehension of the most urgent issues posed by the economic aspects of this crisis. While my superiority on this account is something which I have earned by a unique and important discovery in the domain of a science of physical economy, it must be emphasized, for practical strategic reasons, that my advantage on this account is much more a result of the general failure of those who might be considered my rivals in this profession, than my own accomplishment. In the world of fools, I am a man.

To understand the topics which I have brought together so far in this report, we must conclude this report by introducing a summary, if simplified representation of the most significant scientific implications of my discovery, and point out those of its implications which are of paramount relevance for the subsuming subject and assigned mission of this report as a whole.

The branch of scientific inquiry which reflects both truthful universal physical principles and also those social principles we may properly associate with principles of Classical artistic composition, is the science of physical economy, as I have improved qualitatively upon the original discoveries of the founder of this branch of science, Gottfried Leibniz. The history of that discovery of mine has a homely aspect. This aspect touches upon the nature of the distinction between the pompous lecturer whose classroom manner implies that his wisdom jumped from the brow of Minerva, and the homely individual whose impassioned, stubborn will developed a discovery from the grimy dirt up.

Start with the grime.

When I had not yet reached 16, my father, an accomplished consultant in footwear manufacturing, threw me into the pond, so to speak, doing Summertime factory work in a shoe factory, where I was initially apprenticed as what is known as a "hand-dinker" at the lordly wage of 25 cents per hour. Diocletian be cursed! It is what his father had done to him, and what he was doing to me.

The relevant point is simply my persuasion then, after a few days, that there must be a better way to do this job. Anyone who has actually done meaningful factory labor, and who is not rendered inert by the experience, becomes the kind of person on whom the institution of the factory suggestion-box was focussed: there must be a better way to do this job, to accomplish this result, to improve the product, and to have the gratifying sense of fun with which a useful form of progress rewards its author.

This effect tends to be specific to that sort of employment, as distinct from the generality of "white collar employment."

My father was a strict pacifist, but tended toward rages. (Over the decades since, I have found rage, ironically, but not actually surprisingly, a common characteristic of pacifists.) When he asked me, one day, how is the work going, I replied that I was enjoying it. He darkened. He became furious! I thought he was about to strike me! He had come from a school of thought in which work was fulfilling one's duty to suffer, and a view in which unpaid time which was unoccupied by such suffering was economically and morally worthless. As Shakespeare put the word into the mouth of Cassius, my father's misfortune was that he, although not without a brilliant, and cultivated side to his intellect, and a technical side, too, also had the ideology of an underling. I was already, by that age, a devout Promethean. I thought of work as an opportunity for making useful discoveries, even if of such minor consequence as "hand-dinking," and had a deep moral commitment to saving my time through discovery of better methods, as precious.

That was the homely kind of adolescent experience which was later reflected in my instant, and justified contempt for Professor Norbert Wiener's notion of statistical "information theory." It was that reaction against what I considered the irrationality in Wiener's argument for "information theory," which led me, from early 1948 on, into 1953, to develop and complete my essential discoveries in a science of physical economy.

Once one has actually made an original discovery of a scientific quality, as I have done in that matter, life thereafter is changed in a special way. One's discovery of principle becomes, in a meaningful part, one's self. It is, as Kepler showed in his **The New Astronomy**, a discovered physical principle embedded as one's efficient intention. The experience of acting under the efficient governance of that intention, shapes one's character and related motives in a deep-going way; the principle, as it develops through experience, becomes a characteristic feature of one's personal character. We come to see every experience in terms of the exhibited reflection of the way our now-familiar principle operates universally.

So, when I see a patch of land-area today, I see its expressed relative potential population-density. I see the collective, guilty insanity of the Baby Boomer generation in the collapse of our once productive agricultural and industrial areas, and in the virtual criminality of the asocial effects produced by today's generality of real-estate practices. I see poverty not as personal misfortune of the individual, but as economic folly which is a product of our foolish, current economic policies, for which the nation is now paying dearly in lost real (physical) national income. I also recognize that today's typical Baby Boomers, even presumably well-educated professionals, are simply not capable, in experience, education, or moral conditioning, of recognizing any of the crucial principles on which a successful economy depends. *What a fishbowl mentality they represent! They are, in general, an uncultured generation, of relatively primitive instincts, lacking the characteristics of a culture with economic survival-potential. As the history of legislation and voting shows, they usually prefer bad policies, even very bad policies, over even simply decent ones. Looking back across known history, they represent the cultural potential of a self-doomed culture.* As a qualified economist, with many decades under my belt, this kind of evidence proves conclusively that, unless the trend of our Baby Boomer generation is changed, and that radically, soon, this nation will not continue to exist in a recognizable form. They are living, mentally, in a "fishbowl," and the contents of the fishbowl are about to be dumped, you probably know where.

In a science of physical economy, the apparent division between art and science is dissolved. In physical science, the sovereign powers of hypothesizing of the individual mind, are juxtaposed, experimentally, to nature as represented by the combined abiotic and living domains. In Classical art, and in the politics which is properly informed by Classical art, the individual's sovereign powers of hypothesizing are focussed upon the subject of task-oriented relations among the individual members of a society considered more or less as a whole. In physical economy, these two departments are united, in practice, as one. The science of physical economy is both a physical science and a science of art.

For example, in Classical drama, such as the tragedies of Aeschylus, Shakespeare, and Schiller, the competent author is definable as one who has always recreated a specific page of history to be performed and observed on the stage of the audience's imagination. Any drama must be costumed—if anything other than ordinary street-clothes of today are worn—according to the actual costuming of the period and place of history referenced, and must never be represented as anything but as a true representation of the historically specific characteristics of the culture of that time and place. Any different treatment of a Classical drama is a Romantic's fraud. All Classical art, like drama, communicates by ironical inference, never by symbolism. That is to say, that Classical art, such as a J.S. Bach fugue, or a late Beethoven quartet, is always based on creating a thought-object for which no term exists in the previously established vocabulary. The artist's composition, and its appropriate performance, forces the mind of the audience (and the performer) to generate a definite thought-object (e.g., *Geistesmasse*) which did not previously exist in the vocabulary. The name of the artistic composition then becomes the speakable name for the newly created idea.

The inability to grasp the notion of ideas which function as the equivalent of universal physical principles within the domain of Classical artistic composition, and of statecraft, has the same root as the empiricist corruption which Carl Gauss addressed, in 1799, in his attack on Euler, Lagrange, et al. The denial of the existence of an efficient form of hypothesis, which is the burden of Euler's fraud on the matter of the complex domain, can be, and, in fact, must be traced in European civilization to the attacks on the Pythagoreans by the Eleatics and Sophists, and the attacks on Plato by Aristotle.[13] The empiricists deny the existence of that principle of hypothesis, by means of which, and no other, the experience of a stubborn apparent paradox leads to the discovery of a universal physical principle. Instead of cognition, empiricists insist that all that is knowable must be known by deduction from an appropriate choice of *a priori* assumptions.

Thus, the empiricist, like Thomas Huxley and Frederick Engels, denies the knowable existence of categorical difference between a man and an ape.[14] So, a man from Sun Systems joins the pack of wild-eyed hyenas who insist, as foolish Minsky and Chomsky have followed the clever, but maliciously silly hoaxsters Wiener and von Neumann, in claiming the possibility of building a human mind out of virtual Erector Set parts.

---

13. While many pro-Aristotelian theologians would be angered by hearing me say this, it is a true fact of epistemology, that Aristotle denies the actually knowable existence of either God or a human soul. The result of Aristotle's method, is to transform the word "God" or "soul" from the status of an actuality, to a matter of induced (e.g., taught) belief, to a fantastic sort of Romantic fantasy. This is the same problem expressed by Claudius Ptolemy's Aristotelian fraud against previously known astronomy, and the kindred folly of Copernicus and Tycho Brahe.

14. For example, Euler's denial of Nicholas of Cusa's and Leibniz's proofs of the existence of a well-defined transcendental, and Felix Klein's fraudulent attribution of the discovery of the transcendental to Hermite and Lindemann, are an expression of the insistence of Euler that nothing will be considered to exist unless it is deductively derivable, essentially, from arithmetic. What Euler thus does, as did the Eleatics, sophists, and Aristotelians before him, is the same central argument which Kant, in his *Critiques*, derives from the work of Euler and Lagrange, committing the same error which Gauss, in 1799, points out in the work of the Martinist d'Alembert, as well as Euler and Lagrange.

The same fallacy is the root-origin of the notions of thermodynamical entropy introduced by Clausius, Grassmann, Kelvin, Helmholtz, Maxwell, and the Machian Boltzmann. At the least worst of the work-product of those reductionists, they commit two cardinal acts of scientific incompetence. First, their argument assumes that the universe is primarily, axiomatically abiotic, as the social thought of Bertrand Russell acolytes Norbert Wiener and John von Neumann does. This is the source of their definition of "entropy." They insist on ignoring the fact that the universe is Riemannian, composed of multiply-connected phase-spaces, of which the intrinsically antientropic principles of life and *noësis* are included, efficient intentions (motives). Second, they attempt to measure general thermodynamic processes in terms of Aristotle's impotent concept of "energy," rather than the Pythagorean concept of "power' (*dynamis*). As I have written above, "energy," to the extent it is a meaningful term, points to an effect, not a motive, not an intention. "Energy" is an effect, not a universal physical principle.

In the case of the strictly physical aspect of economy, it is the discovery and application of a universal physical principle, or its technological derivative, which is the only physical source of real profit in the economy as a whole. Furthermore, the real profit of an economy is never competently defined as the sum-total of the profits attributed to local enterprises. Already, with technology expressed at the work-place, we have human passion, human motives. This is the passion associated with the intention to introduce a discovered principle to a physical process.

The silent ("shut up and do your work!") man is never the exemplar of productivity. It is the transmission of motive among people, which is the means by which a principle, discovered by a person, becomes the efficiently motivated practice of many. This motivation depends upon universal principles, which are different than the physical principles of abiotic and living processes *per se*, but are universal principles of the *noëtic* domain.

Take language, for example. Grammar, and, sometimes, even dictionaries, have their uses, but the most important aspects of communication intrinsically violate any fixed doctrines of grammar and dictionaries alike. The generation and communication of ideas respecting principle occurs in the paradoxical features of statements, as the ideas of a Bach fugue illustrate the

The post-modern extreme of empiricism is the "artificial intelligence" fantasies begun by Norbert Wiener (left) and Noam Chomsky (right) of MIT, and opposed by LaRouche since the 1950s. "So, a man from Sun Systems joins the pack of wild-eyed hyenas who insist, as foolish Minsky and Chomsky have followed the clever, but maliciously silly hoaxsters Wiener and von Neumann, in claiming the possibility of building a human mind out of virtual Erector Set parts."

same point (nothing is more hideously inhuman, than hearing a Bach fugue performed without creative insight into the function of irony). Just as an apparent anomaly in the orbit of Mars led Kepler to a uniquely original discovery of universal gravitation, all communication of ideas involves the comprehension of an experienced paradox as a thought-object of the quality of *Geistesmasse*. It is in the psychological tension of experiencing a meaning which exists only as a mocking irony lurking among the cracks of a grammarian's funeral service, that efficient ideas are communicated. It is only in the shared experience of such forms of irony, that discoveries of universal physical principles are communicated among persons.

Hence, as four decades of experience has shown, "programmed learning" is the direct road to intellectual failure, and, often bankruptcy. "Programmed learning" in schools, produces students who pass multiple-choice, computer-scored examinations, without the pains of coming to actually know anything. "Power Point" lectures, thus, spread nothing so efficiently and broadly as intellectual, or, probably, also financial bankruptcy. Communicating only "information," is imparting ignorance, and, sometimes worse, very bad taste.

With those considerations now taken into account,

consider the task of measuring the performance of an economy.

The Reign of Baby Boomer Terror

The Baby Boomer should not be blamed for having been reared to become a Baby Boomer. Our intent should not be to kill him, but to cure him of a condition largely not of his own making. I know, and was watching how and why it happened, while he or she was still young. The real trouble for today's society starts, when the Baby Boomer refuses to admit that he is sick in the relevant sense of that term.

The proper definition of the Baby Boomer, is one born about the time President Harry Truman dropped the bombs and launched a fascist-like right-wing turn in U.S. affairs. The parents of this Baby Boomer had usually been transformed into what I viewed, at the time, as the "stinking cowards" they had become, out of their personal, psychological underling's fear of the Gestapo-like deployments of the Federal Bureau of Investigation (FBI).

For me, for as far back as I can recall, I would have always preferred the risk of death for a good cause, to cowardly dishonor. My policy has been; in dangerous times, always take steps to be certain that you are living, as efficiently as possible, for a cause that is worth dying for. Some regular-guy sort of businessman, the golf fan type, or the late fascist Roy M. Cohn's slimy cousin, Dick Morris—for a case in point—would shudder at the thought that they might be caught dead while visiting a house of prostitution; the idea that their death at the place might appear in the local press, would surely unnerve most of them, as it did Dick Morris. I suspect many of that type have reason to suffer such fears. For me, to be "knocked off" while I might be pursuing a dumb career, has been among my habitual aversions.

Most of the veterans of the war I knew from the late 1940s, were of a different temper. They "adjusted," in the course of time, especially those who drifted into what were ideologically "White Collar" communities, where mothers, especially, taught their children to lie as a matter of policy. "Don't associate with...." "Don't be caught saying...." "Remember, your father could lose his nice job...." These conditions of the parental households and the relevant sort of (especially) "White Collar" communities of the 1950s, produced the likely university-entrant of the middle to late 1960s, who has become the pace-setter core of the Baby Boomer generation, in their late fifties, or early sixties today. A parallel, if somewhat differently colored phenomenon is found in Western Europe. Globally extended contemporary European culture has been polluted by this relatively hegemonic pattern.

The crystallizing factor in the experience of the Baby Boomer generation, has been the relevant events of the first half of the 1960s: the utopians' launching of the Bay of Pigs once Eisenhower was safely out of the Presidency; the utopians' promotion of the hoax known as Rachel Carson's fraudulent **Silent Spring**; the utopians' missile-crisis of 1962; the utopians' assassination of President Kennedy; the utopians' use of the murder of Kennedy as the opportunity to launch the death-trap of what became asymmetric warfare in Indo-China; the utopians' assassinations of the Rev. Martin Luther King and Robert Kennedy in 1968.

These events were situated within the previously prepared context associated with essentially-fascist Fabians H.G. Wells' and Bertrand Russell's launching of a countercultural movement associated with the London Tavistock Clinic; the psychoto-mimetic experiences, under Satanist Aleister Crowley, of the Huxley brothers, Aldous and Julian, and Bertrand Russell's and Robert Hutchins' launching of the Unification of Sciences project, out of which the creators of the doctrine

of "preventive nuclear warfare" launched the pilot forms, during the 1930s and 1940s, of the rock-drug-sex counterculture, "information society," "environmentalism," and similar modes of systemic self-degradation of youth which exploded during the middle to late 1960s.

The combined effect of the induced cowardice, and practiced, immoral sophistry of the "White Collar" climate of the late 1940s and 1950s, intersected the shock of the terror unleashed during the early 1960s, to produce what appeared from the outside to be curiously kaleidoscopic, **Island of Dr. Moreau**-like transmogrifications of the (especially) university-campus-situated Baby Boomers of the period from the middle 1960s through early 1970s. Above all, they were conditioned to hate the blue-collar industrial worker and technologically progressive farmer, and the "industrial society" which that producer represented in their opinion.

Those and related effects on that degeneration of a generation, produced a present-day, ruined, and now bankrupt form of national and (largely) world economy, which has reached the point of disintegrating as before your eyes. The Baby Boomer generation, especially the university graduate who entered what he or she viewed as professional life, was, first, conditioned to, and then became an instrument of the policies which not only caused the collapse of the U.S. and other economies, but have conditioned the Baby Boomer generation of the post-1987 period, into using their rise to top-ranking, or nearly-top-ranking positions of influence, to defend the policies causing the growing catastrophe, rather than correcting them.

With the concomitantly ongoing ruin of the conditions of life of the lower eighty percentiles of family-income groups, and the attrition by death, illnesses, and physical-economic circumstances of the World War II generation of young adults, the stratum of Baby Boomers has risen, which sees itself as "The We Are Wonderful" set, as the necessarily reigning upper twenty percent, the so-called "suburbanite" voter. While their own conditions of life become increasingly precarious, they have generally adopted a device, sometimes referred to as "comfort zones," fantasies into which they flee, in the effort to block out the pains and anxieties caused by the terrible world which they themselves have largely built.

This flight into lunatic "comfort zones" has taken a special form in the Democratic Party, in particular, through the affinity developed with the Fabian fascists of London, gathered around a Cheney-ally Prime Minister Tony Blair, who is, in his own way, not only quite as nasty as Cheney, but actually outranks Cheney in evil on the imperial scale. The indecent union between Blair and the Democratic Leadership Council set, explains much about the way in which the Democratic National Committee has developed a hateful sort of disregard for the welfare of the lower eighty percentiles of the nation's family households, as if to block the view of the world which might be seen from the parapets of the upper twenty-percentiles' "comfort zone" fantasies.

What is shocking in the sheer ugliness of widespread such fantasy-ridden Baby Boomer decadence today, is the indifference to the highly visible rot and doom their generation's hegemony itself has contributed, through its pathetic ideology, to the conditions of life of even those Baby Boomers themselves.

On this account, we need a rejection of monetarism, in favor of my science of physical economy, not only for saving our nation's economy from collapse, but to provide the ideologized Baby Boomer "suburbanite" himself an image of the reality which he must come to accept, if he is not go over, suddenly and whole hog, into something like Nazism, as happened in Germany over the course of the Weimar period.

The Specter of Desolation

Think of the map of the U.S.A. Imagine yourself looking downward from about 10,000 feet above the surface of the land, as you criss-cross the nation's territory, in your imagination. Make a series of such surveys. Make such a trip back to 1933. Try 1940, then 1945, then 1954, then 1963, then 1970, 1975, 1982, 1987, 1992, 1996, 2000, and today. Build up a simulation of a lapsed-time image of the unfolding process of change.

Concentrate on several subject-matters. The condition of forests, fields, and so on generally. Where does the population live? What sectors of the economy are dying, such as the once mighty industrial and agricultural regions? What about the shifting percentiles of relative concentration of the population as a whole?

The image you have, which becomes clearer since about the aftermath of 1971-72, is a destruction of the national economy of the U.S.A., as, now, entire areas have become something like ghost towns, with the population packed, more and more, into more and more densely populated zones of hyperactive futility.

From the standpoint of sanity, which the science of physical economy represents, there are two ratios (think of them as like angular ratios, as in astronomy) which are the paramount parameters of first-approximation physical assessment of a national economy as a whole: physically, what is the state of the economy, and its physical productivity, by area, and as a whole, per square kilometer, and per capita?

Brothers and sisters, our country is dying; it is dying, more and more, and now more and more rapidly, of what has been done to it by our people themselves, over the course of the recent four decades. You, mostly you, above all, have done this to our nation; we have, thus, done it to ourselves.

See what is broke. Fix what is needed and useful which has been broken. Above all, diagnose and uproot those changes in values and mental habits which have misgoverned our nation, and its future, more and more, during the recent forty years. If enough of you disagree with me about this matter, your worries are soon over; you will fairly soon not be around much longer to complain. Perhaps that latter condition is comfort for some our citizens; it will certainly cause them to cease to complain.

CRIMES OF OBAMA

Pakistan's Afghan Border Areas: Victims of Obama's Drone Slaughter

by Ramtanu Maitra

March 25—Months before he was "gifted" with the Nobel Peace Prize late in 2009, President Barack Obama had already begun his cold-blooded killing, using his new-found remote killers, the drones. Years later, in 2015, in his memoir, Geir Lundestad, the non-voting Secretary of the Nobel Committee until he retired in 2014, wrote that he regretted awarding Obama the prize. Lundestad's regret did not bring back to life the thousands that Obama's drones had killed, nor did it help to put back together thousands of families torn apart by Obama's killings, be it in Afghanistan, in Yemen, in Pakistan, or in any other of the seven countries in which Obama and his CIA fellow-killers carried out drone attacks, killing in violation of the sovereignty of those nations and terrorizing their people.

Pakistan's Federally Administered Tribal Areas (FATA) are a case in point. The FATA, a virtually ungoverned area dominated by a string of Pushtun tribes, engulfs border areas of Pakistan and Afghanistan, along the much-disputed Durand Line drawn by the British Raj. In October 2001, soon after the 9/11 attack on the United States, President George W. Bush launched an ill-conceived invasion of Afghanistan, calling it "Operation Enduring Freedom." The goal was to overturn Afghanistan's Islamic fundamentalist Taliban regime, which hosted al-Qaeda and its leader, Osama bin Laden—a largely synthetic figure who has been used to divert attention from the Saudi state sponsorship of the 9/11 butchery. British, Canadian, Australian, German, and French troops joined Washington's Bush-led folly.

Victory is Body-Count

Although the Taliban were dethroned quickly with the help of the Afghan opposition, the FATA territory allowed a large number of Taliban, al-Qaeda, and other local insurgents who had opposed the U.S. invasion, to move into Pakistan and use much of this 10,000-plus square miles of land to set up bases to oppose and harass the invading foreigners in Afghanistan. They began to operate freely, bringing in arms and fighters through the disputed border and ungoverned terrain. It was evident from the outset, that Pakistan had no intention of aiding an outsider nation, such as the United States, to take military control of Afghanistan with its long common border with Pakistan. As a result, whether the powers that be in Islamabad encouraged these fighters or not, the fighters were allowed virtually free movement to carry out their objectives.

By the time Obama was sworn in, in 2009, it was evident

Wikipedia
Barack Obama presenting his Nobel lecture after receiving the Nobel Prize in 2009.

that the Taliban were back in almost full force, and that the so-called "winning" of the Afghan war was merely a dream in the minds of a handful of warmongers in Washington. If he had ever chosen to be honest with the American people, Obama would have admitted that for all practical purposes, all that was left of that invasion was the continued killing of Afghans, while sacrificing more American troops. And he and his fellow warmongers must have known that such killings would create new enemies, possibly more vicious than the ones before. That is exactly what his killing policy delivered in subsequent years.

Nonetheless, mouthing promises of "change," and armed with his Nobel Peace Prize and his drones (first introduced by Bush, but used only sparingly), Obama went about "killing" the "suspected insurgents" from the air, and in the process, killed hundreds of innocent Pakistani civilians, which terrorized the FATA population in general. Such killings of innocent Pakistanis and Afghans were kept under wraps, since no mainstream journalists had any access to the FATA. They were not welcomed in this remote land, which was already very difficult to navigate because of its hilly terrain. Pakistan's authorities, unwilling to abide by Obama's diktats and at the same time afraid of losing arms and aid from Washington, went along with the Obama Administration's official position, re-echoed religiously by the mainstream media, that the drones were killing off only the terrorists (Taliban) and not innocent people.

When Obama saw that he could get away with his killings of "suspected insurgents," he set about to kill his way to a delusional victory in Afghanistan. He launched more strikes in his first year than Bush carried out during his entire presidency. A total of 563 strikes, largely by drones, targeted Pakistan, Somalia, and Yemen during Obama's two terms, compared to 57 strikes under Bush. Between 384 and 807 civilians were killed in those countries, according to reports logged by the Bureau of Investigative Journalism.[1]

U.S. Air Force photo/Lt Col Leslie Pratt

An MQ-1 Predator, armed with AGM-114 Hellfire missiles, in a combat mission over southern Afghanistan.

Pakistan in the Cross-Hairs

According to the London-based Bureau of Investigative Journalism (BIJ), among other sources, Pakistan's FATA have seen the highest number of drone strikes outside of Afghanistan, beginning in 2004. The BIJ calculated that more than 400 strikes were launched targeting the Pakistani Taliban (TTP), al-Qaeda, other foreign jihadist groups, and the Afghan Taliban.

As the CIA began its most intense bombing campaigns in Pakistan between 2008 and 2010, it ignored lessons about minimizing civilian casualties that were becoming critical parts of counterinsurgency doctrine during the same period in Afghanistan. A WikiLeaks cable unearthed by author Chris Woods, a British investigative journalist, noted that the late U.S. special envoy Richard Holbrooke had waved off concerns about the drone strikes in Pakistan with the claim that "drones were more targeted than bombs."

Woods, the author of *Sudden Justice: America's Secret Drone Wars*, has argued that the increase was driven by the desire of the U.S. military in Afghanistan to hit insurgent safe havens across the border. "The many strikes on the TTP, which were not a threat to the United States in Afghanistan, might have been part of a *quid pro quo* deal between the CIA and Islamabad, i.e., the United States struck the TTP in return for Pakistan turning a blind eye to the United States killing those threatening American soldiers in Afghanistan."[2]

1. Jessica Purkiss and Jack Serle, "Obama's Covert Drone War in Numbers: Ten Times More Strikes than Bush," Bureau of Investigative Journalism, Jan. 17, 2017.

2. Cora Currier, "Six Facts from 'Sudden Justice,' A New History of the

Outside a house, withbloodstained walls, after a U.S. drone attack in Mohammadkhel village in north Waziristan along the Pakistan-Afghanistan border. The strike killed about 20 people in two villages..

In Washington, the recurring theme of the Obama Administration has been the alleged precision with which the drones kill. Although since 2001, the United States has asserted its legal right, through an Executive Order signed by President George W. Bush, to kill hostile non-state actors if their host government is "unwilling or unable" to deal with the threat, the BIJ pointed out in its Jan. 17, 2017 report that the Obama Administration has insisted that drone strikes are so "exceptionally surgical and precise" that they kill terror suspects while not putting "innocent men, women, and children in danger." This could be as far from the truth as the United States winning the war in Afghanistan—or the war in Vietnam.

Perhaps more important, Obama ignored the fact that the United States had not invaded Pakistan, but in fact, Pakistan was a partner in America's "war on terror." But Obama, a constitutional lawyer, could not be bothered with those little details. Apparently, to him, remote killing outside of war zones was business as usual. Obama, as President, chose to establish a law only for himself, which would allow only him the power to target foreign individuals, or Americans dwelling in foreign lands, for execution on his sole command, since he determined that the person to be killed was a "terrorist."

The list of whom to kill using drone attacks was drawn up in the White House on "Terror Tuesdays." President Obama, acting as judge, jury, and execu-

tioner, "personally authorized all strikes in Yemen and Somalia and 'the more complex and risky ones' in Pakistan (about a third of the total)."[3]

Micah Zenko, in a 2013 special report of the U.S. Council on Foreign Relations (CFR) titled, "Reforming U.S. Drone Strike Policy," noted that,

Obama Administration officials have also failed to address other troubling questions about the scope of drone strikes. For instance, do legitimate targets include children, individuals attempting to rescue drone strike victims, and the funeral processions of deceased militants? U.S. drones have reportedly targeted all three on multiple occasions.

Presumably, the United States deliberately targets these groups, but when asked, U.S. officials will not acknowledge such practices. In addition, it is unclear if there is a process in place to investigate accidental civilian casualties, hold willful perpetrators of those actions accountable, or provide compensation to the families of unintended victims—similar to the process for accidental civilian casualties as a result of U.S. military operations in Afghanistan. None of these targeting issues stems directly from drones themselves, but instead from the policy choices about how targets are selected, public articulation of who is targeted, and the maintained position that highly publicized CIA drone strikes are covert and thus cannot be acknowledged.[4]

Deny Till the Cows Come Home

What should have disturbed the American people, were repeated denials of drone killings by the Obama Administration, even while many reports emerged in Pakistan on the intensity of the drone attacks. Until 2012, the Obama Administration kept denying that it was killing people with drones inside Pakistan. Such denials also helped Washington to ignore accusations of civilian deaths. In July 2011, the *Guardian* ran an

---

Drone War," *The Intercept*, June 11, 2015.

3. Kate Clark, "Drone Warfare 2: Targeted Killings—A Future Model for Afghanistan?" Afghan Analysts Network, March 1, 2017.
4. Micah Zenko, "Reforming U.S. Drone Strike Policies," Council on Foreign Relations, Council Special Report No. 65, January 2013.

article documenting the strikes on the FATA using the photographs and documents collected by Pakistani photojournalist Noor Behram. Behram is from the FATA, and has documented drone strike scenes in his native Waziristan district.

Sometimes arriving on the scene just minutes after the explosion, he first has to put his camera aside and start digging through the debris to see if there are any survivors. It's dangerous, unpleasant work. The drones frequently hit the same place again, a few minutes after the first strike, so looking for the injured is risky. There are other dangers too: Militants and locals are suspicious of anyone with a camera. After all, it is a local network of spies working for the CIA that are directing the drone strikes.

But Noor Behram says his painstaking work has uncovered an important—and unreported—truth about the U.S. drone campaign in Pakistan's tribal region: that far more civilians are being injured or [are] dying than the Americans and Pakistanis admit. The world's media quickly reports on how many militants were killed in each strike. But reporters don't go to the spot, relying on unnamed Pakistani intelligence officials. Noor Behram believes you have to go to the spot to figure out whether those killed were really extremists or ordinary people living in Waziristan. And he's in no doubt.

"For every 10 to 15 people killed, maybe they get one militant," he said. "I don't go to count how many Taliban are killed. I go to count how many children, women, innocent people, are killed."

According to Noor Behram, the strikes not only kill the innocent but injure untold numbers and radicalize the population. "There are just pieces of flesh lying around after a strike. You can't find bodies. So the locals pick up the flesh and curse America. They say that America is killing us inside our own country, inside our own homes, and only because we are Muslims. The youth in the area surrounding a strike get crazed. Hatred builds up inside those who have seen a drone attack. The Americans think it is working, but the damage they're doing is far greater." ...

There are photos of burned and battered Qur'ans—but no pictures of women: The conservative culture in Waziristan will not allow Noor Behram to photograph the women, even dead and dismembered. So he makes do with documenting shredded pieces of women's clothing.[5]

Kill, But Invoke Law

To escape the blame for the murder of innocent victims, the Obama Administration needed a "legal" sideroad. Jameel Jaffer of the *Guardian*, in a Nov. 15, 2016 article, pointed out that "Senior officials in the Administration of President Barack Obama variously described drone strikes as 'precise,' 'closely supervised,' 'effective,' 'indispensable,' and even the 'only game in town'—but what they emphasized most of all is that the drone strikes they authorized were lawful." In this context, Jaffer noted that "lawful" had a specialized meaning:

> Except at the highest level of abstraction, the law of the drone campaign had not been enacted by Congress or published in the U.S. Code. No federal agency had issued regulations relating to drone strikes, and no federal court had adjudicated their legality. Obama Administration officials insisted that drone strikes were lawful, but the "law" they invoked was their own. It was written by executive branch lawyers behind closed doors, withheld from the public and even from Congress, and shielded from judicial review.

Zenko, in his CFR report cited here, noted that the Obama Administration, breaking with precedent, began to acknowledge the broad outlines of selected drone strikes in early 2012:

> Initially, the Obama Administration maintained that all targeted killings in non-battlefield settings were classified as covert, and officials refused to admit their existence on the record, while candidly discussing the strikes off the record. But in January 2012, President Obama unexpectedly answered a pointed question about drones: "A lot of these strikes have been in the FATA going after al-Qaeda suspects ... actually,

---

5. Saeed Shah and Peter Beaumont, "U.S. Drone Strikes in Pakistan Claiming Many Civilian Victims, Says Campaigner," *Guardian*, July 17, 2011.

allpakistaninews.com

A Pakistani intelligence official reported, on April 22, 2011, that at least eleven people were killed in an Obama Administration drone attack, in which four missiles were fired on a compound in Spinwam, North Waziristan.

placing the napalm or cluster bombs used in earlier days, is that it is much more deniable.

Following that incident, Obama said that Weinstein's family would be compensated for his "accidental" killing. His wife, Elaine Weinstein, made it public that she had been hoping that the Obama Administration and Pakistan's government would together help to free him. While compensating the Weinstein family was the right thing to do, hundreds of Pakistani civilians killed over the years—of which at least 200 were children, according to the BIJ—were not considered worthy of receiving compensation. Weinstein's case was the first time that the U.S. government has committed to compensate civilian victims of drone strikes in Pakistan.

drones have not caused a huge amount of civilian casualties."

Since the Obama Administration was concealing all the drone attacks in Pakistan until as late as 2012, and never admitted the killing of civilians by the supposedly ultra-precise drones, the question of paying compensation to the families of those killed in the FATA did not arise. But Obama had to give up that bit of charade as well. Although the Pakistanis were never considered worthy of receiving any compensation, a crestfallen Obama appeared before news reporters on April 23, 2015, apologizing for "accidentally" killing captive American aid worker Warren Weinstein, Italian hostage Giovanni LoPorto, and two terrorists who were U.S. citizens.

The al-Qaeda casualties were Adam Gadahn, a Californian who became a prominent propagandist for al-Qaeda, was close to Osama bin Laden, and had a $1 million bounty on his head for treason, and Ahmed Farouq, who was described as a deputy commander in Pakistan. These were, however, not the only American citizens killed by the CIA-operated and Obama-ordered drones. These four deaths brought to seven the number of Americans killed by the extra-judicial power grabbed by Obama, while the U.S. Department of "Justice" under Obama's friend, Eric Holder, stood on the sidelines cheering. In reality, the reason that drone killing became the favorite annihilation weapon of Obama, re-

'Grievable' and 'Ungrievable' Lives

Obama's compensation of some, while ignoring others, shows the truth of Judith Butler's analysis that nations at war divide the world into "grievable" and "ungrievable lives." In her 2016 book, *Frames of War: When Is Life Grievable?* She pointed out that lives not considered grievable become targets for annihilation in order to protect those lives that are "worthy of life." Butler further notes how populations who do not conform to Western norms of what it is to be human, end up being abandoned, and while these lives may not be physically lost, they are often destroyed. Perhaps no one absorbed this sick concept better than President Obama did.

Despite growing international attention to the Obama-led drone killings over the years, attacks in Pakistan's FATA went on. The last reported attack was on the then Taliban chief Mullah Akhund Mansoor, who was killed last May in Pakistan's Balochistan province close to the Iranian border. What is unusual is that the U.S. military claimed this strike. Following that incident, the then Pakistan army chief General Raheel Sharif told U.S. ambassador David Hale, who visited the military's General Headquarters in Rawalpindi, that the U.S. drone attack on Pakistani soil to kill Afghan Taliban chief Mullah Mansour, was detrimental to bilateral ties. This is really the first time that the Pakistani Army has openly expressed indignation about drone strikes. Since then, no drone strike within Pakistan's territory has been reported by the Pakistani military.